The Civilization of the American Indian Series
(*Complete list on page 183*)

LIFE AND DEATH IN MILPA ALTA

LIFE AND DEATH IN MILPA ALTA

A NAHUATL CHRONICLE

OF DÍAZ AND ZAPATA

Translated and Edited by

FERNANDO HORCASITAS

from the Nahuatl Recollections of

DOÑA LUZ JIMÉNEZ

Foreword by

MIGUEL LEÓN-PORTILLA

Drawings by

ALBERTO BELTRÁN

Norman
University of Oklahoma Press

By Fernando Horcasitas (translator and editor)

The Aztecs: The History of the Indies of New Spain, by Fray Diego Durán (with Doris Heyden; New York, 1964)

The Olmec World, by Ignacio Bernal (with Doris Heyden; Berkeley, 1967)

De Porfirio Díaz a Zapata (Mexico City, 1968)

Book of the Gods and Rites and The Ancient Calendar, by Fray Diego Durán (with Doris Heyden; Norman, 1971)

Life and Death in Milpa Alta: A Nahuatl Chronicle of Díaz and Zapata (Norman, 1972)

International Standard Book Number: 0–8061–1001–5

Library of Congress Catalog Card Number: 78–177338

Copyright 1972 by the University of Oklahoma Press, Publishing Division of the University. Composed and printed at Norman, Oklahoma, U.S.A., by the University of Oklahoma Press. First edition.

Life and Death in Milpa Alta: A Nahuatl Chronicle of Díaz and Zapata is Volume 117 in *The Civilization of the American Indian Series.*

FOREWORD

Source materials on the Mexican Revolution of 1910 are extremely rich. They vary greatly in type, ranging from ballads and press bulletins to personal memoirs and profound historical studies. Written testimonies are abundant and several bibliographies have been edited on the Revolution, a period that deeply modified the realities of Mexico.

Nevertheless, no one seems to have considered a new type of account: a chronicle stemming directly from the Indian world in a native language, dictated by a person who lived through the events of the Revolution. It might be asked whether a chronicle of this type might lead to a fuller understanding of the struggles which terminated in the social transformation of Mexico. To my knowledge, none of our scholars have come across an account or memoir about the Revolution written in any of the numerous Mexican Indian languages. One person, however, has attempted, with historical and anthropological methods, to gather from modern Indians what might be called their impressions regarding events and situations in their lives during those years of turmoil. I refer to a scholar of Nahuatl language and culture, Professor Fernando Horcasitas, who has begun work in this field, at least in a partial way—partial in the sense that there are other Indian eyewitnesses to the Revolution and that this type of research can be continued while people yet live who underwent the political and social changes of 1910.

Compilation of a memoir of this type is by no means an easy task. The compiler must be familiar with the indigenous tongue. He must know the person who is to act as an informant. It is obvious that he must adopt a criterion enabling him to be free from judgments and prejudices which could lead him astray. Many false steps must be avoided. He must win the friendship of the informant, thus encouraging the free flow of the latter's memories. Once this has been accomplished, he must seek a way of presenting the texts faithfully. The ethnographer will always be exposed to criticism and suspicion. Even if he records his texts on tape, there will always be objections. Did he change the meaning and the feeling of the story? Was he forced to make a final selection of the texts according to his own criterion? And finally, was he in the hands of the "right" informant, who selected certain aspects exclusively and evaluated them according to the anthropologist's inclinations?

To answer these and other questions, the reader must go to the texts themselves, as presented by Fernando Horcasitas in this book. In the most direct manner he tells us where they came from and how they were gathered. He recorded the original Nahuatl texts dictated by an informant in Milpa Alta, a village in the southernmost part of the Federal District, Mexico. He translates them faithfully from the original. The informant was Doña Luz Jiménez; she offers us a personal vision of the Revolution With no preconceived pattern and few value judgments she has created a series of sketches occasionally remarkable in their vividness.

The compiler has divided the texts into two parts. In the first, Doña Luz tells us of her childhood. On reading her words, we are transported back to the times of Porfirio Díaz. We read of her personal experiences and of the life of her community. These first chapters constitute a moving account of bright and dark days in her childhood.

The Nahuatl texts that make up the second part refer entirely to the period of the Revolution of 1910. The protagonist, Emiliano Zapata, is always in the limelight. Because of the freshness and simplicity of the informant, dramatic moments flash throughout the story. Perhaps this image of things past attains a forcefulness to be found in indigenous texts of the sixteenth century: the Aztec memories of the Spanish Conquest, a cycle which I have entitled *The Vision of the Vanquished.*

This life history from Milpa Alta, covering the last days of Porfirio Díaz and the Zapatista revolution surely presents a literary form almost unknown in Mexico until the present. Here is the voice of the Indian world that speaks to tell us of its experiences and attitudes at the flood tide of the Mexican Revolution. There is still time to seek out other eyewitness accounts like this in the same Nahuatl language or in Zapotec, Mixtec, Otomí, Tarascan, and Maya. This series of texts is therefore presented with the hope of stimulating a keener awareness of the Indian's attitude toward the still debated realities of Mexico's social revolution of 1910.

MIGUEL LEÓN-PORTILLA

Institute of Historical Research
National University of Mexico
Mexico City

INTRODUCTION

This work is a collection of Nahuatl texts on the epoch of Porfirio Díaz (1876–1910) and the revolution (1910–19) that overthrew his regime. The story was told to me in Nahuatl, or Aztec, by an inhabitant of Milpa Alta in the Federal District, Mexico—an Indian woman who grew up during the last days of the Porfirian age and who survived the revolutions led by Zapata and Carranza. It is not a history in the usual sense of the word. My informant was not interested in political movements or exact dates. Rather, she wanted to talk about her village and its life in the first twenty years of this century.

Much has been written about the economic, social, and political history of Mexico between 1900 and 1920. Yet no autobiographical work dictated by an Indian in his own language has ever been published. The student of Mexican history, in fact, might find it worthwhile to "participate" in the events of the rule of Don Porfirio and the Revolution through lively narratives written in still other indigenous tongues. One wonders, for instance, how the Revolution of 1910 affected the masses of the Otomí people, hidden among the thorns of the parched wilderness of the Mezquital. What were the reactions of the Maya Indians during the social and political upheaval of Yucatán after 1910? Did the Tarahumara realize that his mountains were contested in the struggle between Pancho Villa and General Pershing? The proud Yaqui who came with Obregón in 1914 to change violently the patterns of life in Milpa Alta —what was his impression of the southern part of the Republic? It will be impossible to answer these questions until we can read accounts dictated by the Indians who lived through the dramatic events of the years immediately before and after 1910. If linguists and ethnographers allow more time to go by, informants and their stories will be gone forever. The man who was twenty in 1910 is eighty years old today.

In addition, this book will furnish the student of modern Nahuatl with linguistic material in a dialect hardly different from that spoken by Moctezuma and Cuauhtemoc. The material is presented here with an English translation that freely reflects the attitudes of the informant.

Milpa Alta, the ancient Momochco Malacatepec, is a

THE FEDERAL DISTRICT OF MEXICO
AND SURROUNDINGS

village lying in the southernmost part of the Federal District, Mexico, some fourteen miles from the Zócalo, the central square of Mexico City.

In 1910, Milpa Alta lay in a sort of no man's land. To the north flourished Mexico City with its half a million inhabitants. Formerly the capital of New Spain, by 1910 it reflected in some ways Paris and New York. One could, however, still paddle south along the Canal de la Viga, as the Aztecs had done, toward the floating gardens of Xochimilco where thousands of canoes still glided with cargoes of flowers and vegetables in what was known then as the "Venice of America." From this lake district, one could ascend abruptly to the craggy mountains of the Teuhtli, the Cuauhtzin, and the immense volcanic range of Ajusco. Between the craters of the Teuhtli and the Cuauhtzin lay Milpa Alta. From there, one could continue to climb to the lofty peaks known as Tierra Fría. There, among the pines and cedars, the eyes of the traveler beheld the South, Tierra Caliente—the lands of Tepoztlan, Cuernavaca, Cuauhtla, and in the distance the stark mountains of Guerrero. These worlds—Mexico City, the lake villages, the mountain towns, and the Hot Country to the South—all will appear in our story.

Because of its peculiar geographical position, Milpa Alta was destined to play an extraordinary role in the Revolution of 1910, when the village became an intermediate point between the hordes of Zapatistas in the South and the military regimes which controlled Mexico

City. In our pages will appear and reappear the phantoms of Porfirio Díaz and Emiliano Zapata and thousands of dead warriors and peasants—Zapotecs from Oaxaca, Aztecs from Guerrero, Otomí from Hidalgo, and Yaqui tribesmen from far-away Sonora.

In 1916 the village was totally abandoned by its inhabitants. The houses were destroyed or had crumbled; the villagers who had not been slain were scattered; grass covered the cobblestone streets. Indeed, according to the informant, the place became the rendezvous of a couple of lost souls who haunted its ruins.

One of the survivors of the tempest that swept over Milpa Alta in 1916 was a woman named Luz Jiménez. It was my good fortune, in 1949, to meet Doña Luz in the home of the anthropologist Robert H. Barlow. Later, she was to be my informant for several courses in the Nahuatl language at the University of the Americas in Mexico.

Doña Luz Jiménez was born in Milpa Alta in the last decade of the nineteenth century. In her early teens, she decided that her mission in life was to become a schoolteacher. She dreamed of herself as an educator of future generations of "professors, priests, and lawyers," an ambition never to be fulfilled.

She remembered with love and gratitude her home, her church, and, above all, her school. She married and had a daughter. In our conversations she often mentioned her mother, who died in Milpa Alta in 1960 at the age of 102.

Between 1911 and 1916, the family of Doña Luz

suffered the violence of the war between the Mexican capital and the southern states, then dominated by Zapata. Later, her village, like many others in Mesoamerica, was invaded by hordes of northerners. She helped bury the bodies of her father and almost all of her male relatives after the massacre of 1916. She was present when the northerners tried to strip "Our Mother," the patroness of the village. And she took part in the nocturnal flight of the villagers when the town was finally abandoned. Her family returned to live in Milpa Alta after Zapata's death in 1919.

During the renaissance of Mexico's mural paintings, Doña Luz posed for a number of famous artists, among them Diego Rivera and Jean Charlot. Her portrait is still vivid on the walls of the Ministry of Education, on those of the Auditorium of the National Preparatory School, and in the Tlatelolco market scene in one of the corridors of the National Palace in Mexico City.

During the last five years of her life, Doña Luz lived in Mexico City with her daughter and grandchildren. She died in an accident in 1965 and was buried in the cemetery of Iztapalapa, near the Capital.

Some years ago, I asked Doña Luz to dictate in Nahuatl the story of her life. For two years we met twice a week, and the pages of this book began to take form. The first edition, published in Nahuatl and Spanish in 1968, was issued by the Instituto de Investigaciones Históricas of the National University of Mexico.

Doña Luz was gentle, unpretentious, and patient with

the *Caxtilantlacame* (non-Indians) who struggled to learn her language. Her personal opinions were never violent, in spite of the tragic events through which she had lived. She spoke Nahuatl and Spanish equally well. All her story bespoke its authenticity; I never found any serious discrepancy in her narration.

According to Doña Luz, there were three great men in the history of Mexico: Porfirio Díaz, Justo Sierra— Díaz' minister of education—and the revolutionary Emiliano Zapata. She never met her first two heroes, but it was her fate to know the third. Porfirio Díaz was "Our Little Father" in Mexico City, the man who taught the people a new and "correct" way of life, the man who created the modern era. Justo Sierra was the man who symbolized to her what she hoped would be her future mission as a schoolteacher. She learned to read and write, thanks to his vision of a new generation of young Mexicans. Emiliano Zapata was "the only man who fought for the poor" and "the first great man to come to speak to us in our Nahuatl language."

Luz Jiménez' trio of heroes may seem fantastic, but if each of us were to write our own list of heroes in the history of our country, our choice might seem even more fantastic than that of Doña Luz.

Before and after our sessions, Doña Luz made comments in Spanish on the story she was relating. These were never transcribed in Nahuatl, but they will appear occasionally in this English version.

The order in which the texts appear in this publication is somewhat different from the way in which they were dictated. I have placed them in a chronological sequence. The punctuation and division into chapters are mine, as are the introductory words at the beginning of each chapter. Although the original in Nahuatl was transcribed in phonetic characters, for typographical reasons it now appears in the traditional Nahuatl alphabet.

The reader will find an appendix containing a glossary of Nahuatl terms at the end of this work.

I am grateful to Miguel León-Portilla of the National University of Mexico for his interest in publishing the first Spanish edition of this work and to the University of Oklahoma Press, whose enthusiasm has made the chronicle available for the first time to the English-speaking reader. My heartfelt thanks also go to Ruth Parlé Craig of the College of Santa Rosa, Santa Rosa, California, whose revision of the entire English text amounted to a most valuable collaboration.

FERNANDO HORCASITAS

National University of Mexico
Mexico City
January 3, 1972

CONTENTS

Foreword   *page* vii

Introduction   xi

PART ONE: THE VILLAGE

I. The Village I Remember   3
II. The Mountains   9
III. The Feats of Tepoztecatl   15
IV. The School   21
V. The Proper Way of Life   31
VI. The Priest and the Doctor   37
VII. Wild Game, Firewood, and Mushrooms   41
VIII. The Miraculous Lord of Chalma   53
IX. Santa Marta and the Day of the Dead   75

X. Moslems and Christians   87
XI. The Good Teachers   99
XII. The Centennial   109

PART TWO: THE REVOLUTION

XIII. The Men of the South   125
XIV. Zapata's Lieutenant   131
XV. The Tempest   137
XVI. The Men of the North   143
XVII. The Fate of the Priest   153
XVIII. Zapata Is Still Alive   155
XIX. The Massacre   159
XX. Flight   165
XXI. The Struggle for Life   169
XXII. Till the Last Cartridge is Gone   173
XXIII. The Return to Milpa Alta   177

Glossary   180

Map: The Federal District of Mexico and Surroundings   xiii

PART ONE: THE VILLAGE

Ompa nochan, Momochco Malacateticpac, tlaca tequiti ihuan cihuame tlaxcaloa, tlacualchihua. Oncuan on
yecoz tlacatl ye mayana nochi tlacuali za tequichia. Ihqui
in ica nemia nochantlaca.

Noca yahue tlaca tequitizque cihuame noihqui tlacoa
ompa tianquizco campa monamaca nacatl, yetl, tlaoli—
nochi tlen monequiz—cuahuitl, tecoli, xochicuali: nochi
in itech monequi cihuame ipan cali. Yomocuepque
cihuame tianquiztli quitlipantlalia tlacuali ihuan huici.
Quizaca atzintli ica ce ticaxalotin nozo tepozcaxtin ihuan
tla yohuala tenamic, tzicuini cihuatontli quicoaz neuhtli.

Iqui in, temachtiani, niauh nimitztlanonotzaz inin tlatoli
itech naltepeuh ihuan nonemiliz.

Momochco Malacateticpac, naltepeuh, itocan Milpa

I. THE VILLAGE I REMEMBER

We are in 1905. Don Porfirio Díaz reigns in Mexico City as an absolute ruler. Not far south of the Capital, Milpa Alta, still a mixture of Pre-Columbian and Spanish culture patterns, has not been affected seriously by the progressive spirit of the early twentieth century.

Our informant, who lived in this Mexican village in 1905, tells us about her people.

In my town of Milpa Alta men used to work and women made tortillas and cooked the food. So when the husband arrived home hungry, his meal was waiting for him. That is the way the people of my village lived.

While the men were off at work, the women went to the market place to buy things. All the necessities were sold there: meat, beans, corn, firewood, charcoal, fruit—all a woman needs at home. When the women returned from the market place, they set food on the fire and cooked it. They brought water home in large pots. So it was, when the husband got home, his wife ran to buy him his *pulque*.

And so, professor, I am going to tell you a few words about my village and my life.

Momochco Malacatepec, my village, is called Milpa

Alta caxtilancopa nozo Asunción Milpa Alta ihuan intzalan tetepeme Cuauhtzin ihuan Teuhtli.

Nota, nonan, cuali otlatoaya macehualcopa ihuan
caxtilancopa [. . .]

Achtopa inin tlatoli itech notatzin niauh nitlanonotzaz.
Icuac nehua nitepiton notatzin ayemo huel omotequitiliaya. Zan yehuatl omotlaquichiliaya cuentla matlactli huan
ome metoton huan omotlachiquiliaya oncuan on mochi-
huaz neuhtli. Ican ayemo miac tepilhuan oyeya cuali opanoaloya ica neuhtomin. Ipan on tonaltin ipatiuh ce *litro*
neuhtli yeyi *centavo*. Ica ipan tica on amo omopiaya *litros*
que axan. Ica tlatamachihualo iman tica on oyeya almon-
tin tlacualmon ihuan *cuarterón*.

Ica on omopanoltiaya notatzin ihuan nonantzin. Zan
niman oyecoque tepilhuan. Ye timiactin. Ihuan nocnehuan
otiyeya tichicuacentin. Ye yiman tica on ocuache notatzin
omotequiliaya ocuache ipampa ye timiactin otiyeya ipan
cali. Notatzin omopiliaya tlen motequitiliz tecuecuentla.
Yomiquiliaya *arado*, yomotequitiliaya tlaltepoztli. Noihqui quemanian omotequitiliaya ica tlalacha; inon ica
metzontequiquixtilo ihuan tlaltepoztli ica omotocaya
tlaoli. Ihqui on ic omonemiti notatzin. Oncuan on aic
otechpolo tlen ticuazque, tlen tiquizque; nian noihqui
totzotzoma aic otechpolo.

Ye yiman on notatzin omaniliaya tequitl que inon
mitoa ica *estajo*. Ihuan oncuan cuali motequitiliz omeuh-
tzinoaya yeyi *hora* huatzinco; nicaz motlatlalhuiz tlaoli,
nozo mepopohuiz, nozo mometzontequixtiliz. Ihuan icuac

4

Alta in Spanish—or La Asunción Milpa Alta—and it lies between the mountains of Cuauhtzin and Teuhtli.

My father, my mother, they spoke both Nahuatl and Spanish well. It was very different in those times. No one was ashamed to speak Nahuatl. Many people did not even speak Spanish.

I have seen many good things and many bad things in my life, but what I loved most was when I was a little girl and started going to school.

But first of all, I am going to tell you a few words about my father. While I was still a very small child, my father did not have much work to do. All he did was work his twelve *maguey* plants out in the fields for their pulque. At that time we were not many children, and we could live on the money he got from the pulque. In those days a liter of pulque cost ten centavos. But we did not use the word "liter" as we do today. It was just a *cuartillo*, a half of a cuartillo and a fourth of a cuartillo.

My father and mother could live on that. But then more children came. We were many. Now we were six sisters, and my father had to work harder because we were now so many in the house. My father had to work in the corn-fields. Sometimes he worked the plow; other times he worked with his hoe. And there were times when he worked with his axe. With this axe he would uproot the maguey plants, and he used his hoe for sowing corn. And that was my father's life.

5

aciz chihnahui tlatepoztlamachotiloni notatzin yomocen-
cahuili ce *tarea*; zan niman omaxitiaya calitic; yecan
almazal. Omamazalhuiaya ica ye moli nozo chilatl ica
nacatl ihuan omitiaya ineneuhtzin.

Zan niman omaniliaya mecapali ihuan *hacha*. Omiquili-
aya itacatl para ome tonali, neuhtli noihqui ome tonali,
atzintli ica mopozoniliz icafentzin ompa cuautla. Noca
moxexelhuiaya cuahuitl oncuan on metequechiliz *horno*
oncuan quizaz tecoli. Iman yometequelic omocauhtzino-
aya ce yohuali ihuan cemilhuitl. Oncuan on mohtiliz tla
oticuic nozo oceuh *horno*. Ipampa iqui on quimati quichihuaz *horno*; tlicui ihuan cehui; ihuan tla ocehuia notatzin omomectliquechiliaya.

6

So it was that there was never anything wanting in the way of food and drink, nor in clothing either.

Then my father got work as a day laborer. In order to do his work well, he would get up at three o'clock in the morning. He would go off to cultivate the cornfields or to work the maguey plants or to tear out their roots. By nine o'clock in the morning, my father had already finished his labors. Then he came home, and his breakfast was waiting for him: boiled beans or meat in chile sauce and a little pulque.

And then sometimes he would go off with his leather tumpline on his forehead and with his axe. Then he would take enough food for two days, enough pulque for two days, and enough water to prepare coffee out in the woods. Once he had split all the firewood, he would build a rock-oven to make charcoal. Once he had the oven working, he could stay out in the woods a day and a night. He had to keep watch over the fire, to see if it was burning or not.

The fire would catch sometimes and then go out. And if the fire went out, my father would start it over again.

Tlanonotzalo ipan tepetl Tehhuehuentzin huan nochtin tetepeme tlen techmalacachoa in ompa Momochco Malacatepec. Inin Tehhuehuentzin techmononochiliaya tocoltzitzihuan hueyi momamalito que in tlatoltin in tetepe. Ompon mochihua tlen huehueyi tlaca, mahuiztiquez: tepatiquez que non mitoa, inon quincuitia tlamatquez. Ihuan icuac aca mococoa quitoa, "Tiahue topopoazque ca xihuitl nozo ca totoltetl." Yehuan tlon ompon yauh quintepehuazque totoltetl nozo xihuitl ica tetl itocan chalchiuhtetl; campa metztica Tehhuehuentzin.

Ihuan inimequez tetepe nochtin antica yencuic tlaxcol ica Cuauhnahuac. Ca ce otli itzintlan Tehhuehuentzin huan yauh aciz Cuauhnahuac. Metztica ompa occe huey tlamacatzintli: occe *lado* metztica impan in xolal in Tepoz-

II. THE MOUNTAINS

To the north, in the direction of Mexico City rises the holy mountain, the Teuhtli, the Old Lord. And to the east sleeps Iztaccihuatl, the White Woman, who separates Milpa Alta from the Valley of Puebla.
There are legends about these mountains.

Many things are said about the Mountain of the Lord Teuhtli, and about all the hills that surround us in our village of Milpa Alta. Our ancestors claimed that the Teuhtli was the greatest of all the mountains. Illustrious men, wonderful men were trained there, witch doctors and healers. When someone is ill, people say, "Let us go cleanse ourselves there with herbs or eggs!" There, where the Teuhtli rises, people go to offer herbs or eggs, together with stones called jade.

All these mountains are linked underground as far as Cuernavaca. There is an underground passage which goes from the Teuhtli all the way to Cuernavaca. There is also another magic mountain: the great Lord Tepoztecatl, who lives on the other side, near the lands of Tepoztlan; he too

tlan Tlatihuani noihqui mahuiztictlacatl Tepoztecatl. Inintzin tlatihuani no hueyi tlamatcatzintli. Miaque tlaca Momochco Malacateticpac ohuilaloya Tepoztlan monamacaz cuahuitl. Zan niman huitz; can metztica huey tlamatque in Tepozton.

Zan niman in Popocatepetl; noihqui ce huey tlatihuani. Ompon omocochititoc huan icihuahuatzin icxitlantzinco metztoc. Itocatzin Iztaccihuatl nozo Malintzin.

Inin Iztaccihuatl tlanonotzalo mach oconmotitlaniaya momepiliz; oquimixotiliaya cuacuetin, metoton, cahuatin. Quenon omometztequitiliaya. Huan ican cihuapili, cuali conetl, mahuizticcihuatl, cualtzin; nochi ixaxayacatzin cuacualtzin cihuaconetl.

Inintzin tlatihuani oquimochihua oquimonochililiz itlactzinco mocihuauhtitzinoz in Popocatepetl. Zan niman oquimolhuili Iztaccihuatl: "Nian tehuatl, nian amaca; niaz nicochiz. Tinechixotiz." Huan neci zan omocochitiz. Omotecatzino in cihuapiltepetl mocochitiz ihuan Popocatepetl quimixotilica.

Zan niman icuac omotac ye yehuatzin yompa metztica tetotopixqui.

"¡Malintzin, Malintzin!" quimolhuilia in teopixqui, "¡Ximehua, ximehua! ¿Tlen ticchihua? ¿Tlica ticochi?"

"Nehuatl amo ninehuaz," ohualnanquili Malintzin. "Axan nian nochan. Axan xinechehuacan tla nanchichicahuaque. Nonamic, inin tlatihuani, oquinec nian nicochhuetziz huan nian nicochtaz. Niquixotiz nochtin xolal. Oncuan niquintlalpoliuh tlen quizque, tlen quicuazque

10

is a great wise man. Many people of Milpa Alta go to Tepoztlan to sell firewood. They come back, after they have visited the wizard Tepoztecatl.

Then there is the Popocatepetl, the Smoking Mountain, who is also a great lord. There he sleeps with his wife at his feet. She is known as Iztaccihuatl—the White Woman, Mariquita.

People say that the White Woman was once a shepherdess; she tended cattle, sheep and horses. This herdswoman was gentle, beautiful, like a fairy—a good girl. Her face was lovely.

And the lord, the Smoking Mountain, asked her to become his wife. But the White Woman answered, "Neither you nor anybody else. I am going to sleep, and you will watch over me." And it seems that she fell asleep. The Virgin Mountain lay down to sleep and the Smoking Mountain watches over her.

After they had talked, a priest suddenly appeared at her side.

"Mariquita, Mariquita," the priest says, "Rise; get up! What are you doing? Why are you asleep?"

"I am not going to get up, for this is my home." Thus answered Mariquita. "If you feel so strong, why do you not try to lift me? My spouse, this Great Lord, wanted me to go to sleep, and here I will sleep. I will watch over all the lands of the village. From here I will see that people have enough to eat and drink; and all of them will have to meet sometime with the Teuhtli. Behold, there go all the shep-

huan nochtin nenanamicoz Tehhuehuentzin. Ompoyon metzticate nochtin memepixque, tlen onechmixotilique huan axan quimixotilia metoton, inin metoton, icuac pehua quiahuiz huitze, icuac huitz tecihuitl; yehuan in quincuitia 'tlamatquez metoton'."

herds on their way. Once they watched over me, and now they care for their sheep. When it is about to rain, when it is about to hail, the sheep feel it coming. That is why they are called wise sheep."

Inin oyeya ce cihuapili ompa Tepoztlan. Ce momoztla
oyaya tlapacaz achi miac tzotzomatli. Ompa atlaco otlacuaya. Oquihuicaya itacatl; oncuan on tla yomayana
otlacuaya.

Inin cihuapili achi cualtzin, cualtzin ixayac ihuan iyolo.
Ompoyon oyaya momoztla tlapacaya ica panoz.

Amoca oquimatia tla ompa oya ica ompa on ichpocatl
oquitaya papanototol ica iyixpa. Amoca ipan omomatia
tla oztopa yeyecame ompoyon. Icuac oquitaque ichpocatl
ye cocoxque. Ichan yotlacualania tlilcan ihqui on ipan
omochiuh.

14

III. THE FEATS OF TEPOZTECATL

Contacts between Milpa Alta and the Hot Country, especially Tepoztlan and Cuernavaca, are perhaps more frequent than with the Mexican capital. In six hours on foot, the men of the village cross the mountain range to sell their firewood in Tepoztlan. Because all speak the same dialect of Nahuatl, friendships are easily born between the men of the Federal District and those of Morelos. The weary woodcutters of Milpa Alta return to their homes satisfied after their long walk and bring long and fantastic tales to tell—tales about the country to the south. One of them deals with the deeds of the Tepoztecatl, legendary hero of Tepoztlan.

There was once a maiden who lived in Tepoztlan. She went every day to the river to wash clothes and she ate there. She carried her food with her, and when she became hungry, she would eat.

The maiden was beautiful—a comely face and a good heart. And so, she went every day to the river to wash clothes and to make her living in this way.

No one really knew what was happening down there, at the riverside, but the young woman kept seeing a little bird which flew around her. No one knew that there was a cave there, inhabited by the winds.

15

Tatzintli de nichpocatl omoteniquili itlac ce caxtiltecatl aquin oquimolhuilic: "Mochpochtzin ya quipiaz ce cone-tontli. Nimitzmotlatlauhtilia amo timaguiliz; ihuan conetl icuac yecoz ticmotlazotiliz. Hueyiyaz ihuan timotiliz tlen ipatiuh piltzintli."

Ihquin omochiuh: amo quimagayan cihuaconetl. Icuac oquipix conetl ye tlazotli. Ohueyac ihuan omochiuh telpocatl.

Huan ohuala opaxaloco ica Mexico. Yehuatl oquitleca-huitl tepoztlatzilinali ca *catedral*.

Icuac ohuala Mexico oquinhualmamatac itic huacali ome palomaxtin. Ihuan yoyaya ica Tepoztlan occepa ica cuauhtlatli. Omocehuitl piltontli; ican yauh ciauhtaya tepitzin omotecac. Hueliz amo cuali oquitzatza huacali. Oquizque palomaxtin. Huan omotlalique: ce icpac teo-pantli Tepoztlan ihuan occente icpac tepetl can chanti Tepozton.

Zan niman oquimati telpocatl que inantzin yauh monamictiz. Ye yiman teopa calaquiz opeuh yeyeca; ihuan omopachoc in Tepozton itlactzinco topixque. Quimol-huilia: "Amo tiquinmocencahuiliz ican cihuatontli quipia notelpochton." In topixque amo omotlaneltoquiti. Oqui-mocencahuilic ihuan oyaque ichan cihuatzintli Ompoyon otetlaitilo. Ichan telpocatl otlacualo. Iman ye tlacualoz omopachoc Tepozton huan quilhuia: "¿Tlican otimona-mictic? Ye hueyi totelpoch ihuan otimitzpanoltiani tone-huan."

16

Eventually, the girl was known to be pregnant. At home her parents were furious when they found out what had happened.

But the father of the girl had a dream. He saw a well-dressed young man, a city fellow, who told him, "Your daughter is about to become a mother. I beg you not to beat her. When the child is born, you will love him dearly. He will grow up and you will find out his true worth."

And so it was. The girl was never beaten, and when the baby was born he was much loved. The Tepoztecatl grew up and became a young man.

One day he came to visit the city of Mexico. With his great strength, he managed to lift the bells of the Cathedral into their places.

When he came here, he was carrying with him a crate containing two doves. But on his way back to Tepoztlan by the mountain, the youth stopped to rest. Because he was tired, he lay down to sleep a while.

Perhaps he had not closed the crate well, because the doves got out.

One went off to sit upon the church of Tepoztlan and the other upon the hill which is the home of Tepoztecatl.

Later the young man learned that his mother was going to be married. When she was ready to enter the church, a frightful wind began to blow. And the young Tepoztecatl went up and spoke to the priest. "Don't marry them because the woman is the mother of a son of mine." But the

17

Amo tlananquili cihuatontli. Opeuh zan niman yeyeca. Oquihuicac ipan oyitic yecamalacatl; oquintlecahuitl icpac tepetl campa momati chanti Tepozton.

priest refused to believe him. He married them, and everyone went off to the woman's home, to the wedding feast. And the young man was invited to the feast. When they were about to eat, the Tepoztecatl approached the woman and said, "Why did you marry? Our son has grown up now, and we would have spent our lives together with him."

The woman did not answer. Then a furious wind began to blow. And this whirlwind carried them off to the top of the mountain where, as we know, the Tepoztecatl dwells today.

Ica ipan in tonaltin amoca huel oquinequia quihuicaz in ipilhuan ompa tlamachtilcalco ipampa ahueli quintzotzomatizque achi cualtzin. Inchachan onemia tzotzoyoquez, tzatzapaltiquez; zan ompa omahuiltitinemia pipiltoton ca ipan otli nozo oyatinemia ica cuecuentla.

Ipan ce cali ometztaya ce cihuapili omomachtiaya momachtitzinoz, mopohuiz amatl. Omotemachtiliaya ipan icaltzin. Tatatzin ahquehuan oquinequia ixtlapohuizque ipilhuan; otlaxtlahualoya ce tomin *cada* piltzintli nozo cihuaconetl momachtiz.

Itocatzin Malintzin; tenamic itocatzin Mauro Melo. Noihqui oquinmomachtiliaya pipiltoton. Itic on tlamachtilcali onohtiti niquiixmatiz ce, ome, yeyi *letra* ihuan ihqui cuiloz noihqui nitlapoaz.

IV. THE SCHOOL

In 1905, in the nearby Capital, Porfirio Díaz appoints Justo Sierra as head of the Ministry of Education. Sierra's enthusiasm for rural education is contagious. He pioneers the rural federal school—free and obligatory. The instruction of children is not to be limited to the three R's, nor to the walls of the classroom. It is a social process which must transform all the ways of life of the new generation. A small private school already exists in Milpa Alta, but in 1905 the federal primary school is founded.

In those days almost nobody wanted to send his children to school because they could not dress well enough. Dirty and in rags, they lived in their huts. The children only ran about in the streets or in the cornfields.

In the village there was a good lady who knew how to read, and she taught in her home. Parents wanted their children to learn how to read; they paid a *real*, twelve and a half cents a month, for each boy or girl who went to study there.

The lady's name was Mariquita, and her husband was Mauro Melo. He also taught the children. It was in this school that I learned a few letters and that I learned how to read and write.

Later my mother told me about how I used to cry be-

21

Nonantzin nechmononochiliaya quename onichocaya ipampa onicnequia nicalaquiz tlamachtilcalco; ye yiman on ayemo huel miaque oyeya temachtiquez. Nonantzin onechmomatechanilitaya ihuan otitaya tianquizco. Ihuan ican otipanoya ixpan on cali otitaya omahuiltiaya cocone nozo quema nian omomachtiaya. Nehuatl onichocaya; onicnequia nicalaquiz noihqui nomachtiz. Nichocaya coza ipampa onicnequia nicmatiz tlen quitoa amame, inon tlacuiloltin. Ayemo huel nihueyi; onicpiaya chicome xihuitl. Nonantzin amo omonequiltiaya niaz itic tlamachtilcali ipampa nitepiton ihuan nechtlacalizque occequi coconetoton. Can nozo amo huecauh nonantzin ihuan notatzin ica nichoca onechhuicaque itlauhtzinco cihuapili in omotemachtiliaya.

Ye yiman ye nihuehueiton notatzitzihuan onechmiquilique ompa tlahueimachtilcalco. Amo oquinequia nechanazque ompa nomachtiz.

"Tetepiton cihuatontli," oquito in *inspector*, "xicuicacan namochan ce xihuitl ipan in nancualicazque. Ye tamechanilizque ma ocuachi huepahui. Tlacamo oncuan chocataz."

Nonantzin oquimolhuilic *inspector*, "Mahuiztic tlacatl, huel miac nimitzmotlatlauhtilia ma mocahua nocihuanton. Coza quitequipachoa momachtiz. Ye quiixmati tepitzin *letras*."

"¿Quenin quimatiz?" oquito *inspector*, "Tepitzin cihuanton; ayemo huel hueyi. Namehuan nanquinequi namechaniliz namoconeuh. Xiccaquican: tla ticanazque

cause I wanted to go to school. At that time there were not many teachers in the village.

My mother used to take me by the hand as we went to the market place. But when we passed the teacher's house, we saw the children studying or playing. I used to cry because I wanted to be one of the students, too. I cried because I wanted to know what was written on the papers. I was not a big girl; I was seven years old. My mother did not want me to go to school because I was small, and the other children might knock me down and hurt me. But since I kept crying, my father and my mother soon took me over to the teacher's home. Later, when I was older, my parents took me to the big school. But they did not want to accept me.

The principal of the school said, "You had better take this little girl home and not bring her back until a year from now. We will accept her then, when she is older. Right now she will do nothing but cry."

"But, sir," my mother said to the principal, "I beg you to allow my child to stay. She likes to learn. She already knows a few letters."

"How can that be?" the principal said. "She is still only a child; she is still very small. But you want me to accept your little daughter. Listen then: if we accept your child, you will have to bring her here at eight o'clock in the morning. The bell will ring, and she will have to go inside with all the other children. You will have to come get her at noon and bring her back at two-thirty. Don't think she is

cihuanton nanquicahuaquihue nican ipan chicueyi tlamachotiloni. Tziliniz tepoztli yeyez calitic campa nochtin
cocone yezque; ihuan nancanaquihue tlaco tonali. Occepa
hualaz ipan ome huan tlaco tlamachotiloni teotlac. Amo
xiquitocan zan yehuatzinco momachtiz. ¿Tlen nanquitoa?
¿Nanquicelia nozo amo?"

Notatzin ica nonantzin omitlahuique ma iqui mochi-
huaz. "Ticahuaquihue yehuatzinco ihuan ticanaquihue
ican tlacuatiuh, ihuan zatepa hualaz momachtiz ica
teotlac."

Omotlatlanique notatzitzihuan, "¿Quexquich titlaxtla-
huazque?"

"Amitla," otlananquili *inspector*, "amo tlaxtlahuazque
cocone ican momachtizque."

Ye yiman on otlatlanihuac, "¿Tlen ticualicazque ica
tlacuiloz, tlen amochtli, tlen ocuache timotlaniz oncuan on
moztla cualicaz noconeuh?"

Iqui otlananquili *inspector:* "Amo, amo tlacualicaz. Tla
melahuac quitequipachoz momachtiz oncuan ticmacazque
amatl ihuan nochi tlen quinequiz. Oncuan quinmatizque;
ica teotlac quititizque tlatzomaz, tlatetequiz ihuan occequi
tlamahuizoltin. Zan yehuatl hualaz chipahuac in tzotzoma,
chipahuac itzonteco. Amoca cualicaz yolcatl icuac ticpac
ihuan tlacahhuiz; amo hualaz *sin* cahtli. Iqui in motitizque
quename nemizque icuac ye huehueyi."

Opanoc xihuitl ihuan onipano quilhuia ome xihpa
nomachtiz.

Iqui in notatzitzihuan onechmomachtilique.

going to study only in the morning. What do you people say? Do you accept my conditions or not?"

My father and mother accepted. "We will come to bring her here early and take her home at dinner time. Then she will come back to study in the afternoon."

"What is this going to cost?" my parents asked.

"Nothing," the principal answered. "Children don't have to pay anything to receive an education."

"Then," my parents asked, "what kind of writing material is she going to need? Or which book? What should our daughter bring tomorrow?"

But the principal answered, "Nothing, nothing is to be paid. If it is true that she wants to learn, we will give her paper and everything else. Here we will teach her how to read, and in the afternoon to make dresses and many other fine things.

"But I warn you that she must come in a clean dress, with her hair washed and free from lice. And she must wear shoes. She must not come to school barefooted. In this way, children will learn how to live properly for the time when they are grown-ups."

A year went by, and I entered the second grade at my school.

This is the way my parents gave me my education.

Around the year 1908 I entered a school called Concepción Arenal, which was housed in one of the homes of the village of Milpa Alta. The principal and the inspector lived in the upper story. The name of the principal was

Ica ipan in xihuitl mitoa *novecientos* chicueyi onicalac ipan tlamachtilcalco itoca *Concepción Arenal* Momochco Malacateticpac. Ompa chantiaya tlacpac *director* ihuan *inspector*. *Director* itoca *Lucio Tapia* ihuan *inspector* itzonquizca *Guzmán*. Oncuan on nochipa cualcan oquitlapoaya tlamachtilcali. Icuac onipeuh momachtia temachtiquez oyecoya ompa Milpa Alta. Queman chicnahui tlamachotiloni huan tlaco. Zan nohuian omonemili quename inin tlamachtilcali hueyi oyeya, oquitlauhqueque quen caltin can chantizque temachticahuan. Xexelihca oyeya.

Ye yiman tica in nochtin piltzitzintin oquipiaya tlen yezque ixpan tlamachtilcali quemen chicome huan tlaco tlamachotiloni yehuatzinco, icuac otzilinia in tepoztli. Ye yiman on piltzitzintin otzicuinia nochtin cacizque in *lugar*.

Ye yiman tica on tatzitzintin opaquia ihuan oquitoaya: "Iquin in zan cualcan hualazque cocone. Quema cuali momachtizque, cuacuali cocone quizazque ipan inin tlamachtilcali."

Ihuan omolhuiaya tatatzitzintin: "Amo timonequiltiz motelpochtzin nozo mochpochtzin oncan temachtiz noihqui?"

"Quenin amo," molhuiaya "zan huel nechpactiz."

Otomachtiaya ocpac cemilhuitl ihuan ahquen amo cuicaya icac quename on petlantaz, nozo amo mamohuic, amo motzocuazhui, oquititlania ipan tlamachtilcali can momachtia pipiltoton. Ompa pipiltoton oquixopapacaya,

26

Lucio Tapia and the inspector's last name was Guzmán. The doors of the school would open early. When I began to study there the teachers would arrive in Milpa Alta at around nine or nine-thirty in the morning. But soon it was agreed that since the building was large, living quarters could be arranged for all the teachers.

All the children had to be standing in front of the school by seven-thirty in the morning when the bell rang. It was then that all the boys and girls ran to take their places.

By this time the parents had been pacified and thought, "Our children will have advantages this way. If they learn their lessons well, good sons and daughters will come out of this school."

And the parents were asked, "Would not you like your son or daughter to become a teacher here like us?"

"Of course," they answered, "we would like that very much!"

We studied twice a day and the girls who went to school wearing dirty shoes, unwashed and unkempt, were sent to the boys' school. The boys washed their feet, combed their hair and shined their shoes with a grease called *bola*. Thus, with a rag, they polished the girls' shoes till they shone. In this way we were taught to live a proper life; it was a terrible shame to have the boys comb and wash one's head. Once they had been washed they were taken back to the school of Concepción Arenal.

oquitzocuazhuiaya ihuan icahhuan noihqui oquintlapal-
huiaya ica quicuitaya *bola*. Ica ce tatapatli oquipopoaya
can quizaz tlapetlanali. Iqui on ica otechtitique quename
ica tinemizque. Ican tepinauhtin quename pipiltoton
otetzcuazhuiaya oteamohuiaya. Tla yoquinmamahuique
oquinhuicaya occepa tlamachtilcalco *Concepción Arenal*.
Yeca ipan *novecientos* chicueyi iqui in otechtitiaya que
tinemizque cuali.

Ompa Milpa Alta amo onyeya atl. Ohuilaloya Nochcalco tlapacoz cequi tlacatl. Ohuilaloya noihqui tlapacoz
ica *San Gregorio* Atlapulco; occequi ompa Tecomic. Iqui
on otechpiaya tichichipahuaquez. Tatatzintli omehuaya
queman nahui tlamachotiloni ica ce cahuayo huan cui-
tlaxtli oyaya quicuizque atl ompa Nochcalco. Yehuatl on
otiquia ihuan ica otlacualchihualoya. Opapanoc iqui in
tlen omotetequipano.

Totlamachtilcahuan amoca huel oquinequia mocahuaz
chantiz Momochco Malacateticpac. Amo onyeya caltin
quintetlaquehuizque; amo inyeya pantzin. Nian aca tlate-
palehuiz. Nochtin temachtiquez amo oquinequia moca-
huazque. Oncuan on omonemili oquintlaquehque caltin.
Ye yiman on opehque mocahque temachtiquez Momochco
Malacateticpac.

All this took place in the year of 1908, when we were first taught to live properly.

There was no water in Milpa Alta. Some people went to do their washing in Nochcalco. Others went to wash in San Gregorio Atlapulco and others in Tecomitl. Thus we managed to keep clean. The father of the family rose at about four o'clock in the morning, mounted his horse and carrying a leathern sack, went off to bring water from Nochcalco. The water was used for drinking and cooking. Our water problem was solved in this way.

Not one of our teachers, not one of the *señoritas*, was willing to stay overnight in Milpa Alta. There were no lodgings for them, no wheat bread and no servants. None of the teachers wished to live there. But now they began to rent houses, just as had been planned by the authorities of the village. So it was that the teachers began to stay overnight in Milpa Alta.

Iman imahtzinco *general* Díaz ompa Momochco oyeya altepetl quicuitiaya *prefecto*. Yehuatl on ma mitoz oquin-mandaro ya oquinmandaroaya in altepetlaca.

Inin ipanoc ca yipan *novecientos* chicnahui iman on nehuatl niluz Jiménez onicpiaya cana matlactli xihuitl.

Ye yiman tica in imac Totatzin Porfirio Díaz; tlaca zan omotzotzomatiaya icoton ihuan icaltzon. Ihuan oquitoaya *prefecto*: "Noihqui namechilhuia namehuan aihmo nicne-qui nanquiztinemizque ica caltzon. Nicnequi ye namo-

V. THE PROPER WAY OF LIFE

We are at the beginning of the twentieth century, when Victorian norms (or Porfirian, in Mexico) are a model for the only "proper way of life" for the entire world. In one way or another, the new Mexico must conform to European patterns. Don Porfirio, the educator Sierra, and the evolutionist philosophy of the time demand that older ways of life—Aztec and Spanish—be abandoned in favor of progress. It becomes "improper" for a man to be seen in the short white pants of Spanish times. It is improper for girls to attend school without stockings. It is improper for boys to walk barefooted. It is improper to speak Nahuatl, when Spanish has become the language of the nation. Milpa Alta reluctantly accepts Progress and becomes more "proper and correct" every day.

But not all the villages of Mexico share the evolution of Milpa Alta. Farther south, beyond the Cuauhtzin, in the Hot Country, live thousands of Indians without long trousers, without shoes, without schools, and without Spanish.

But that is another story. Let us return to Doña Luz.

In the times of General Díaz, a judge ruled over Milpa Alta and he was called "The Prefect." He was the one who governed the people of the village.

All these things happened around the year 1907 when I, Luz Jiménez, was about ten years old.

In those times, when Our Father Porfirio Díaz ruled over the country, the men of my village wore only their shirts and short white pants. But the judge used to admonish them, "I have already told you that I do not want

machtizque quenin yezque ipan in xolal. Tla oncate cocone nanquititlanizque tlamachtilcalco ihuan nanquipatlazque namotlaque. Tla amo nanquipia tepilhuan zan xihpatlaca namotlaquen. Ahquen amo tlaneltocaz ce metztli motlacalilia; oncuan quinchazque. Ye cuali ye necohuiloz tlaquemitl."

Oquinemilique *prefecto* ihuan *inspector* quintzatzacuazque nochtlaca quipiaz nozo amo quipiaz iconeuh. Quipiaz tlen tzauhtaz queniman quitlatolanazque huan tlananquiliz tlen quitoa iyolo. Quintitlaniz tla quintitlanizque inpilhuan tlamachtilcalco. Aquen otlanaquiliaya quititlaniz ipilhuan tlamachtilcalco oquincacahuaya. Ihuan tlen oquitoaya amo oquipiaya tlen tzauhtazque ce metztli. Ihuan oquimilhuiaya: "¿Quezqui cocone nanquimpia? ¿Nanquititlanizque tlamachtilcalco?" Occequi oquitoaya: "Amo nicpia cocone; zan nocnehuan." "¡Can nozo xiquilhui motatzin ma quintitlani tlamachtilcalco! ¡Amotla tlaxtlahuazque!"

Ye yiman tica on ometztac tlatihuani Justo Sierra, *Secretario Educación*. Omotemaquiliaya amoxtin ica momachtizque cocone ihuan amatl ica tlacuilozque. Amotla omocoaya. Nochi on oquitemacaya ompa tlamachtilcalco ihuan zan yehuatl yazque chichipatique cocone. Tlen *primer año, segundo, tercero* ihuan *cuarto* zan yehuatl omomachtiaya otlapoaya huan mocuicatiaya. Tlen mitoa *quinto* huan *sexto* omomachtiaya amatl ihuan tla cihuantoton oquinmachtiaya tlatetequizque, tlacuicuiloz-

you to wear those short white pants. I want the people of this village to learn how to live in a better way.

"If you have children, you must send them to school and you must also change your way of dress. And if you don't have children, it will be necessary for you to change just your way of dress. If you don't obey, you will be caught and put in jail for one month. It's about time you bought modern clothing."

The judge and the principal decided to jail all the men of the village whether they had children or not. The men were imprisoned in order to be questioned and were kept there until they had given an honest answer. They were asked whether they were willing to send their children to school. Those who answered "yes" were freed. And those who claimed that they did not have any children were locked up for a month. They were questioned, "How many sons and daughters do you have? Are you going to send them to school?" Some answered, "I do not have any children—just brothers and sisters." "Well then, tell your father to send them to school. It won't cost them a cent!"

At that time, Señor Justo Sierra was the Minister of Public Instruction. He gave the children books to study in and paper to write on. Nothing had to be bought; everything was free at school. They only requested that children come to school neat and clean. Those in the first, second, third, and fourth grades were taught just to count and sing. We who were in the fifth and sixth grades studied out of

que cuali tzotzomatli ica *máquina*. Otechititiaya noihqui titlacuicuilozque itech amame. Noihqui otechnonotzaya totemachticauh quenin ica omochihuaya pantzin.

books, and the girls were taught to cut dresses and embroider pretty clothes on the sewing machine. We learned how to draw pictures on paper. And our teachers also taught us how to make wheat bread.

Ometztaya ompa Momochco ce topixque itocatzin
Juan de Polo, mexicatlacatl. Oquimpiaya ome icnehua: ce
itocan Conchita, occe Elenita. Yehuan in omochantiliaya
ompa teopantli. Inintzitzin cualtin mahuiztic cihuame
omotetlacoliliaya tlacuali tlen icnotlacame.

In topixque Juan de Polo omochilhuiliaya yeyi *misa*
ipan *domingo* ihuan ica *semana* ome ipan macuili tlapoali
huatzincotica. Nahui tlamachotiliztli otenotzaya teteachca.
Icuac tziliniz macuili tlapoali ye yiman on moquixtiaya
topixque ica itzotzomatzin oncuan ye pehuaz moteochi-
huaz *misa*. Ipan *semana* oyeya ome *misa* huan ce *rosario*
ipan teotlactli chicuacen tlapoali.

Achton topixque—amo nictocamati itocatzin inintzin
topixque—icuac yehuatzin ometztaya ipan teopantli omo-
tectitili quenin ca netocoz. Oncuan achtocopa zan ica

36

VI. THE PRIEST AND THE DOCTOR

And there are also a priest and a doctor in Milpa Alta.

Juan de Polo was the priest of Milpa Alta, and he came from the Capital. He had two sisters, one named Conchita and the other Elenita. These three lived on the church grounds. These good ladies gave away food to the poorest people of the town. Father Juan de Polo said three masses on Sundays and two during the week, always starting at five o'clock in the morning. At four o'clock, the sexton began to ring the bells. When the bells were about to sound five o'clock, the priest appeared in his robes and the mass began. During the week, there were two masses daily, and the rosary was said at six o'clock in the evening.

The priest who was in charge before—I do not remember his name—taught the people of the village how to bury the dead properly. Before his time, the dead were buried wrapped up in old mats, and thus they were interred.

petlazoli; oquimoquimilhuia miqui huan iqui on ohuilaloya ica quitocazque.

Oncuan oacic tonali topixque quinmolhuilia tlaca ihuan
cihuame: "Axcan namotequipachozque: nanquipiazque
quezqui tomin ipampa ye cuali mochichihuazque caxatin,
ma zan que *colmenas* caxon. Aihmo netocoz miqui ica
petlatl." Omotlanonochili topixque quename miqui *sa-
grado* quename teotatli. "Ipampa on namechilhuia ma iqui
on ca netocoz."

Noihqui topixque Polo oquinmononochiliaya nochtin
tlaca ica cihuame quename motocaz ce miqui ihuan iqui
omochiuh.

Totatzin Polo hueyi omotemaquixtili. Coza cuacuali,
tlatoli omotlanonochiliaya. Ica on oyolehuaya toyolo.
Amo quimectiliaya ipampa topixque oquimopatiliaya
chantlaca tla aca amococoz. Amo patio otlaxtlahualoya,
zan ome tomin. Huan tla icnotlacatl amo tlaxtlahuaya nian
ce *centavo*. Topixque oquitlacoliaya ichantzinco tlacuali
tlen quicuaz cocoxqui. Iztayotl *hasta* cempoali ihuan matlactli tlaca. Momoztla mocuitiuh iztayotl ica cuanacanacatl ihuan tlaxcali. Omotlanahuatiliaya topixque: "Momoztla tihualaz, nanchi, ticuicaz itlacuatl motatzin. Icuac ye
cehuiz aihmo tihualaz."

Ica on amo oquimotlazotiliaya Basurto. Inin tlacatl
hueyi tepatiqui ipan toxolal. Oquitlania ome *peso*, ome
peso ihuan nahui, macuili; tla techanmicaz omotlaniaya
matlactli *peso*. Ican cuali tepatiqui amo oteyolcococuaya
tlaxtlahualoz.

38

So it was that the day came that this priest told the men and women, "You should be concerned over this matter; you should have a little money put away to have coffins made—even if they are as cheap as the boxes used for beehives. I do not want the dead to be buried wrapped in mats." The priest explained that the dead body was sacred —something almost divine. "That is why I tell you to bury your dead properly."

In later times, Father Polo also told the men and women how they should bury their dead, and it was done.

Our Father Polo was the salvation of many people. His kind words filled our hearts with joy. If someone in the village was sick, the priest went to heal him. He charged only twenty-five centavos, a very reasonable price. And when he went to visit a sick man who was poor, he did not charge one centavo. From his home, he gave away food for the sick: broth for as many as twenty-four persons. Every day people went to his home to get the broth, chicken, and tortillas. And every day the priest would say, "My child, you must come here every day to take food home to your dear father. When he gets well, you will not have to come again."

Because of all these things, Basurto did not care for the priest. This man was the highly respected doctor of our village. He charged two pesos or two pesos and a half, and if he went to the sick one's house, he charged ten pesos. Because he was a very good doctor, people were not sorry to pay his price.

Itech cuauhtlatli Momochco Malacateticpac *hasta* itech Ajuscotepetl-inimequez tetepe nochipa tlacelic ipan in cuauhtlatin. Ica on nochtin tlaca ica cihuame iqui inic omopapanoltiaya. Cihuame tlen inmoquez aihmo oquipiaya inamic oyaya cuauhtla xoletemozque, ye on oquinamacazquia ipan tianquiztli. Tlen tomin oquiquixtiaya itech xoletl yehuatl onica oquimpanoltiaya icnotzitzin. Inimequez cuauhtincihuame ican achi oquintlazotlaya inpilhuan ocualicaya xoletl ihuan icuaticpac tepitzin cuahuitl ican oquintlacuachihuilizquia tepilhuantoton.

Ihuan tlaca itech Tupilejo ihuan Cuauhtzin itechcopa San Pablo Oztotepec noihqui oquiquixtiaya in nelhuayo ocotl ihuan tlachpahuaztli inon quicuitiaya popotl. Noihqui inin popotl oquimano ochichihuaya ihuan ocualnama-

VII. WILD GAME, FIREWOOD, AND MUSHROOMS

Although the people cultivate their fields of corn and century plants, the mountains give them game, firewood, and mushrooms.

From the woods of Milpa Alta all the way up to the peaks of the Ajusco, the forests are always damp. And men and women made a living from them. Women who did not have a husband went to the woods to gather mushrooms to sell in the market place. With the money they obtained for the mushrooms, they managed to support their orphaned children. These women of the woods loved their children dearly; therefore, they brought down some mushrooms and a little firewood in order to provide for them.

The men of Topilejo and the Cuauhtzin, which lies on one side of San Pablo Oztotepec, also gathered *ocote* roots and the broom plant called *popote*. They made bunches of this popote and took them to sell in the city of Mexico. Others sold them in Milpa Alta. They also brought twigs

caya ompan Mexico. Occequi zan ipan ompa Milpa Alta oquimanamacaya. Noihqui ocualicaya tlacotlachpahuaztli. Tlen achto otenehque tlachpahuaztli in popotl ica otlachpanaloya ipan calitic ihuan tlaco tlachpahuaztli ica mochpanaya nochi caltemitl den cali. Iqui on opapanoaloya tlaca ihuan cihuame.

Noihqui tlaca oquimacia mamaza, totochtin, teporingo; noihqui yepatl ica tepatiloya inomequez necocoloya itech toyezo. Oquincuacualachiliaya; amo oquitlaliliaya iztatl. Quiltequiciayo cocoxqui inon tlen icohuicia yepanacatl ihuan quicuaz tepitzin nacatl. Noihqui tlacamo tzopiniaya ica acoxa ihuan itech iman ocalaquia ica in yolcatl in nacayo nozo icuitlaxehuayo. Zan quitlalilizque zan campa oyeya acoxa ihuan oquiquixtiaya. Iqui on ic oquimpatiaya achtocopa.

Noihqui oquitlacalia ipan cuentlatin tocazque tlaoli, yetzintli ihuan ahuax. Yehuatl on momacehuitazque nochi in xihuitl noca yahue quitomozque tlen quinamacazque Tupilejo, San Pablo Oztotepec ihuan San Salvador Cuauhtenco. Oquitocaya miltin, chicharonmiltin, colextin ihuan oquitemohuiaya Xochimilco. Nochi ohualnamacaya. Ica on oquicentlaliaya in tomin quemanian ic oquicoaya cahuatin. Quemanian ic oquicoaya tlaltin. Quemanian ic otlalprendanaya. Iqui in ic opapanoya tohuanpotzitzihuan.

Ipan in cuauhtlatli itech Momochco Malacateticpac onyeya miaque cuauhtin ihuan tlaca miactin oyaya cuacuahuizque. Oquimamayahuia cuauhtin. Ye yiman tica on amaca oteahuaya nozo otetzacuaya ipampa momamaya-

to make brooms. The popote brooms were used to sweep the inside of the houses, and the twig brooms were used for sweeping the yards. In this way men and women made a living.

Men also hunted deer, rabbits, and *teporingos*, as well as skunks to cure those who had diseases of the blood. The skunks were boiled without salt. The sick person had to drink the broth in which the flesh of the skunk had been boiled, and he had to eat a little bit of the meat.

Furthermore, if someone got a needle stuck in his hand, the needle could be extracted with the meat or skin of this animal. Those were the methods of healing in those times.

People also sowed corn, beans, and lima beans in their fields. These they could sell all year round at Topilejo, San Pablo Oztotepec, and San Salvador Cuauhtenco. They sowed fields of peas and cabbage and took them to Xochimilco. They took all these things to be sold at the market. At times, they saved enough money to buy horses. Other times, they bought lands. Still other times, they rented out their lands. This is how our neighbors made a living.

In the woods of Milpa Alta grew many trees, and many men went there to gather firewood. They felled many trees. In those times, nobody minded or put one in jail for cutting down trees. There were many trees, and the poor people ripped the branches off the fallen trees. And if a man wanted his wife to sell firewood in the market place, he brought home the wood already split. He would load two horses and a donkey; the donkey would carry the fire-

43

hui cuauhtin. Ixachi miaque onyeya inimequez cuauhtin.
Nochtlacatl tlen icnotlaca oquimatzatzayatzaya inomequez
yohuehuetztaya cuauhtin. On tla oquinequia cuahuitl
oncuan quinamacaz icihuauh ipan tianquiztli, ocualicaya
tlaxexeloli. Quitlamamaltia ome cahuatin ihuan ce axno,
oncuan on axno oquimamaya cuahuitl tlen omonequia
ipan cali. Iqui in miaque tlaca oncuacuahuia ipan on
cuauhtlatli. Oyeya ahuacuauhtin, ilcuahuitl, tamazquicua-
huitl, ococuahuitl ihuan tepehuexocuahuitl.

Itech in cuauhtin quename ocotl ohuepahuia ce xiuhtontli coza omonamacaya tianquizco ihuan oquicuitiaya
"ocoxochitl." Mopozonia ihuan miac tlacatl quename
desayuno ica tlayia.

Occente xiuhtontli itoca tlaloreganillo; noihqui mopi-
piaya icuac cehua aca moticocoa. Oquipozoniliaya ihuan
tototonqui oquipiaya tlen quiz cocoxqui.

Noihqui occequi cuauhtin oquitemacaya quename ilitl
quitemaca ce xochicuali chichiltic ihuan tzopelic. Cuali
mocua.

Inahuacuahuitl oquitemacaya; inon oquicuitiaya "ahuatzapotl." Icuac ohuetzia ahuatzapotl hualaya inon oquicuitiaya caxtilancopa *bellota.* Technonotzaya quename
cuali omochihuaya que *café.* Omocequia ihuan omoticia
ihuan oquineloaya ica tepitzin *café* tlen ocualnamacaya
tepoztlantlaca.

Noihqui tlaca ontochacia oquimamaya tepoztlacue-
poniloni ihuan quimaci totochtin mamaza ihuan occequi

wood which was to be used at home. So it was that many went to get firewood in the forest, where there were oaks, birch, madrone, berry trees, torch pines, and willows.

Upon these trees, such as the ocote pine, there grew a small plant—a parasite—which was sold in large quantities on the plaza. It was called the "flower of the ocote." Many people boiled it and drank it for breakfast.

There was another herb called *tlaloreganillo*. This was also kept carefully in case someone had a stomach ache. It was boiled, and the sick man had to drink it hot.

Also, there were other trees such as the birch which produced a sweet, red fruit. This could be eaten.

The oak gave a fruit called *oak zapote*. When this oak zapote fell, it had acorns inside. We were told that they could be made into a kind of coffee. They were toasted, ground, and mixed with a little of the coffee which the men of Tepoztlan brought for sale.

Men also took their shotguns and hunted rabbits, deer, and other small animals called teporingos. This type of game was and still is eaten in our village.

Under oaks, ocote pines, and birch—under all these trees—mushrooms grew. The mushrooms began to sprout in the month of May. At that time of the year, they were very expensive since they were difficult to find in any other place. In Milpa Alta, mushrooms were sold in large quantities. Some people also went out to dig up the roots of the ocote pine from which they made hand brooms. And at the

yolcatoton ocuachi tepitoton oquincuitiaya "teporingos." Inimequez yolcame omocuaya ihuan mocua.

Noihqui itzintla ahuacuahuitl ihuan ococuahuitl ihuan ilcacuahuitl—nochtin in cuauhtin itzintla—otlacatia xoleme. Opehuaya xoletl oquizaya ipan metztli *mayo*. Iman on coza patioquez ican ayemo huel cana oyeya. Xoleme coza omonamacaya ompa Momochco. Occequi tlaca oconquixtiaya inelhuayo ocotl ica oquichichihuaya tlapapaxelhuaztin. Ihuan itzintla in ococuahuitl otlacatia xoleme coza chichipahuaque, achi cualtzitzin, noihqui huelhuelic.

Xoleme noihqui oquizaya nanacame, tlacananacatl. Omoticia, omotlacaliliaya chilchotl ihuan tepitzin yepazotli. Itzintla ailcuahuitl otlacatia occequintin xoleme quincuitiaya chilnanacame.

Notatzin omonemitiaya ipan cuauhtlatli ihuan nochtin xoleme oquinmixmachiliaya. Ce tonali ohualmiquili tochan chilnanacatl ihuan ce tlacananacatl. Inimequez ome xoleme ocualicaya miquiliztli ipampa oquimamatocato coatl. Huan omiquilic oncuan techmotitilizquia oncuan tiquiiixmatizque xolet: tlen cuali mocuaz ihuan tlen ocuicatza miquiztli. Omotetequilic ica tepoztlatlateconi ipan ce huepali huan otechmolhuili: "Xihualaca, xiquitaqui ihuan xiquixmatican tlen amo cuali xoletl ihuan tlen cuali mocuax." Inin xoletl tlacananacatl ihuan chilnanacatl oxoxoqueque ihuan zatepa oxoxoqueque quiltontiquez.

Iqui in nochtin tlaca yomohtitiaya tlen cuali ihuan amo cuali xoletl. Oncuan on aihmo ca ocuicaya ichachanton

foot of the ocote trees, the mushrooms grew very clean, very beautiful, and very tasty.

Other mushrooms grew. They were called *nanacatl* and "male mushroom." These were ground up, mixed with green chile sauce, and were seasoned with a little *epazote* herb. Under the birch trees another mushroom grew, the *chile* mushroom.

My father worked in the woods, and he knew all the mushrooms well. One day he brought home a chile mushroom and a male mushroom. These two are deadly when they have been touched by a serpent. He brought them home to teach us about mushrooms, to show us which ones can be eaten and which ones bring death. He placed them upon a board and cut them with a knife. "Come and see!" he said. "You will know the difference between bad and good mushrooms." Soon the male mushroom and the chile mushroom turned blue, and then they turned green. This meant that they would bring death.

So it was that all the men learned how to tell the good mushrooms from the bad. Therefore, nobody took home the one which brings death. But some still wondered, "How can we tell which mushroom brings death?"

One evening, many men were sleeping in the forest. And the man who was to bring them their food had not arrived. They all said, "Let's go gather mushrooms! We still have two or three tortillas for each of us. We are getting hungry, and we have nothing to put inside of the tortillas."

Two or three men went off to gather small mushrooms.

47

xoletl tlen ocuicaya miquiztli. Ihuan ye yiman motlatlania:
"¿Quen ica tiquiixmatizque xoletl inon cuicatz miquiztli?"
Ican miactin tlaca ompa ocochia cuauhtla. Ihuan ce
tlacatl ahquen oquihuicaya in tlacual amo acito. Yiman
tica on quitoa nochtin: "Tiahue tictemoa xoletl. Oc topilia
ome nozo yeyi tlaxcali. Yauh pehuaz timayanazque ihuan
antlein tlen ica ticuamanazque totlaxcal."
    Ome que yeyi tlaca oquitemoto xoletl, inon tzitziquitzin.
Ihuan occequi omotlalique quicuiquilia tlali tlen itech
ohualaya in xoletl. Occente tlacatl oquitlalic tzitzintli; occe
oquipapac xoctli tlen ica pozoniaya atlapozon ica tlayix-
que. Inin xoctli ican hueyi ihuan miaque xoleme onyeya
oquixnenehuilique quename itic on xoctli nochi xoletl
cuali huiciz ihuan conehuiz oncuan tlacuazque nochtin.
Oquipaque in xoletl zan niman ihuan ye cuacualaca atl
oquitetepehque itic xoctli xoletl. Oncuan on icihcan
huiciz. Ye yiman conmati tla yohuicic, ye yiman on ye
cuali mocuaz. Oquitlalilique chilchotl, xonacatl ihuan
yepazotli. Oncuan on ahuiyac quizaz tlacuali.
    Oyeya ce tlacatl amo huel opaquia iyolo quicuaz xoletl.
Zan iyolo oquilhuiaya: "Ah quimati cuali xoletl ticuazque
nozo ahquen miquiz." Iman tica on otlato tlatihuani:
"Amo ximomauhtican, amo ximomauhtican: xoletl ticuazque nochi cuali."
    Yiman tlaxexeloa nochtin oquiquixtique in tlaxcal.
Ihuan tzatzi nechca, "Ye huitz tlacualero." Cuicatz totlaxcal; axan tectlacuazque.
    Inon ce tlacatl amo yolehuia iyolo achi omoyolcocuaya

48

Others sat down and brushed the earth off the mushrooms. Another man started a fire. Still another washed the pot in which the coffee was boiled. Since this pot was very large, the men succeeded in putting in enough mushrooms to feed them all. When the mushrooms had been washed and the water was boiling, the men put them into the pot so they would be cooked rapidly. Then they bit them to see if they were well cooked and ready to eat. They added green chiles and onions and the epazote herb. This was going to be a very tasty meal.

But there was a man present who was not at all eager to eat the mushrooms. Deep in his heart, he felt, "Who knows if these mushrooms are really safe to eat? I wonder if any one will die?" Then another man said, "Don't be afraid. Don't be afraid. We are going to eat good mushrooms."

Suddenly one of the men yelled, "Here comes the man with our food and more tortillas! We will eat well today!" Then tortillas were brought out and passed around.

But the man still did not want to eat because he was afraid of being poisoned by the mushrooms. And the man who was cooking the food said, "Sit down. We're going to eat. Nobody is going to die." Then everyone shouted, "Let's see. Let's see what you have thrown into the pot!"

"A peso that did not turn green," the man explained. "The coin boiled with the mushrooms, and I had already washed the peso with soap and straw. And when the water was boiling, I threw the coin in among the mushrooms.

ica mopahuiz ica xoletl. Mahuiztic tlacatl, in oquitlali tlacuali, quitoa: "Ximotlalican; tiahue titlacua. Amaca miquiz." Nochtin tzatzi: "Tla tiquitacan, tla tiquitacan, tlen otimotlalili."

Ihuan opeuh tlacatl: "Inin ce *peso* amo xoxoqueuh. Ocuacualaca itic xoletl. Cual on nicpapac ca xapo ica ichtli in ce *peso*. Iman cuacualaca atl ica xoletl onictlacal inin *peso* itic xoletl. Huan xiquitacan: nian xoletl amo xoxoctic nian ce *peso* amo xoxoqueuh. Inin quitoznequi cuacuali xoleme."

Yompon ohualpeuh zazanili que ica achtocopa omimicoaloya ican amo omixmatia xoletl. Omocuaya zan tlahuiz. Ipampa on netequipacholoya ma cuacuali xoleme yecan. Aihmo aca omiquia.

50

And look. Neither the mushrooms nor the coin turned green. This means that the mushrooms are safe to eat."

People commented that many had died in previous years because they could not tell good mushrooms from bad ones. People ate them foolishly. Today people are very careful to pick good ones, and nobody dies.

Ompa Momochco yexpa xihuitl ohuilaloya nehuentiloz itlauhtzinco in Toteotatzin itocatzin Chalma. Inintzin mahuiztic teotl oconmotlazocamachililiaya ipampa tlaca mococoa, cihuatl nozo pipiltzitzintin. Zan ica oquimotenehuiliaya ocehuihualoya. Ipampa on huel miac tlacatl oquimaxilique ica *devoción*. Ihuan ica on yexpa tlaca xihuitl oanaloya. Cequi tlacatl omohuentiaya candelerotin; cequi tlacatl oquixihquimiloaya achi miac xochitl. Oncuan on acizque ompa Chalma quimotlapalhuizque teotl quimotlalilizque, quimopatililizque xochitl inon yehuahque ihuan quitlalizque inon celic ixitlantzinco in Toteotatzin. Nochtlacatl ocuicaya zazo tlein ompa ixitlantzinco, noihqui *cirios*. Ye on oyaya mohuentizque.

Opehuaya oanazque ipan metztli *enero*. Oyaya miac

52

VIII. THE MIRACULOUS LORD OF CHALMA

Some forty miles to the southwest of the village lies the shrine of the Holy Lord of Chalma, built upon the grotto of Oztoteotl, God of the Cave, an Aztec deity worshipped centuries before the Spanish conquest. It is represented today by a crucifix. Now in the early years of the twentieth century, the people of Milpa Alta go on a devout pilgrimage to offer their love and tears to the Crucified Lord of Chalma.

Three times a year, the people of Milpa Alta went to make offerings to Our Father, to Him who is known as the Lord of Chalma. When men, women, or children got sick, they would later go to thank the good God for their recovery. Whenever one invoked his name, one got well. That is why many loved him dearly. And that is why, three times a year, the people set out on their pilgrimage. Some went to offer him wax candles and candle sticks. Others made little bouquets of flowers wrapped in green leaves. Thus they would go there to Chalma, to visit the God in order to renew his flowers. They would remove the wilted ones and place fresh ones at the feet of Our God the Father. Everyone carried an offering to his feet. And they took candles, too.

tlaca ihuan cihuame mohuentizque ompa Chalma, quin-motlazocamachililizque. Tlaca omococo ihuan oquimo-tenehuili Totatzin Chalma ica nochi iyolo oquimocehuili-aya. Nozo cequi oquintzacuaya nozo oquinmictizquia ichtehquez ihuan zan nica oquimotenehuiliaya Toteotatzin Chalma, oquimocuepililiaya chicahualiztli. Ihuan inome-quez quintzacuiliaya ichtehquez oquinmomaquixtiliaya noihqui. Zan ica oquinmotenehuiliaya mahuiztic teotl ocholohuaya ichtehquez: nian amo quinmacatehuaya, nian amo tla oquiquixtiliaya. Ica on tlaca ompopolahuia ompa itic teocali Chalma.

Inimequez mahuiztic tlaca ihuan cihuame oquichi-huaya itacatl ica tamali, tlatlayoyo ihuan popoyec. Oqui-mamaya patli tla ca mococoz ipan cuauhtlatli, ye on quimacazque. Ica on netlaliloya patli *hasta para* cahuatin ican cehua quimaci itic cocoliztli.

Panoaya ica San Pablo Oztotepec, zan niman San Salva-dor Cuauhtenco, San Miguel Tupilejo. Ipan in xolal noch-tin nenencatzitzintin omotlaliaya tlatotoniloz. Ompoyon momacehuizque ce tlaxcali, nozo ce pantzin ica tepitzin atl apozon. Iqui on ic otlayia tohuampohuan.

Ye yiman tzatzi teecanqui, "¿Ye nochtlacatl omocen-cahualo tlayi? Tlen cahuapahuiloa ma yenetlalilo intzalan huacaltin; ican yotlaihuac tocxanazque achi cualcan taciz-que. Ompa Agua de Cadena titlacuazque."

Opanoaloya ica Tierra Blanca. Zan niman Agua de Lobos. Zan niman opanoaloya Agua Escondida. "Oncuan necxanaloz tlen nenemoa; macamo necahualo tlacuitlapa.

The pilgrimage on foot began in the month of January, when a great number of men and women went to offer their gifts and to thank the Lord of Chalma. People who had been ill went, those who had cried out from the depths of their hearts to Our Father, the God of Chalma, and who had been healed. Perhaps one had been in jail. Perhaps one's life had been threatened by thieves, and upon invoking the Divine Father of Chalma, one's strength had returned; for he was known to save those attacked by robbers. One needed only to call out the name of the good God, and the robber fled; he could not do harm or steal anything. And that is why people gathered in the temple at Chalma.

These good men and women prepared food for the journey: tamales, maize breads filled with beans, and fried breads of unleavened corn. They also carried medicine in case someone became sick on the road. They even took medicine for the horses, because they might get sick from the cold.

They passed first through San Pablo Oztotepec, then through San Salvador Cuauhtenco, and then through San Miguel Topilejo. In the lands of this last village, the pilgrims stopped to heat their food. They ate their tortillas or bread with a little coffee. This was their breakfast.

Then the leader would cry out, "Have you all finished your breakfast? Those who are riding, get back on the crates! Since everyone has already finished breakfast, we

Tonochtin tomanaca; cuachi topan quizazque ichtehquez. Ipan in Agua Escondida huel momati ichtehquez. Ahquen quinequi atliz cuali quichihuaz oncuan achi huehuecaton ca Agua de Cadena."

Ompoyon Agua de Cadena cahuatemoa tlatotonilo. Miactin tlaca quicentlalia cuahuitl; quitlalia *luminarias* can mototoniz tlacuali. Achi cualtzin omohtaya. Nepa, nian, omohtaya cualquixtia tlacuali. Tlen inon tlatiquihuaquez cuicaya cuanacanacatl ihuan huexolotlacuali ica tamali. Ihuan miaque tohuampohuan amotla ocuicaya, nian ce tlaxcali, nian ce pantzin. Oquitlatlacoliaya nepa, nian. Quitzatziliaya, "¡Xicanaqui motlaxcal!" Occe tlacatl cualitoz. "¡Xihuala: occe motlaxcal ica nacatl!" Occequi quitlacoliaya tamali, can pachihuiz ahquen amo cuica itacatl.

Noihqui ocuicaya mohuentiquez tepitzin *aguardiente, anís* ihuan *jerez.* Oncuan on tla mitonitiuh ahquen quiz atzintli itztic quipiaya tlen quitequilizque tepitzin *aguardiente* oncuan on amo mococoz. Ihuan *anís* ihuan *jerez* inon tlen cahuapa. Oyaya cihuame nozo ichpocame ican ahueli ocahuatemoya oquicamamatia in *jerez* oncuan on aihmo huel amiquiz, *hasta* icuac axihuaz campa onca atl. Ye yiman yomocahuatlalique nochtlacatl Minas, cen tetepetl. Inin tepetl ca yihpac Agua de Cadena.

Ahquen amo ca iyolo oyaya Chalma tlalhuiquixtiz tla itla oquipanoaya ipan tepetl.

Tehuan, nonantzin ica ome nocnehuan. Zan oquito occe nocneuh: "Tla onicmatini quename huehca metztoc

are going to arrive early. We will eat our meal in Agua de Cadena."

They passed through Tierra Blanca, then through Agua de Lobos, and then through Agua Escondida. "From here on," the leader said, "those who are walking must hurry. Let no one remain behind. Let's keep together in case of robbers. It is said that there are highwaymen at Agua Escondida. Those who wish to drink water should do so now, because Agua de Cadena is a long way off."

At Agua de Cadena, they got off their horses and sat down to prepare food. The men went to gather firewood. They made bonfires to heat the food. It was a beautiful thing to see. Here and there one could see people bringing out their provisions. The rich brought cooked chicken and turkey and tamales. But many of our neighbors had brought nothing—not even a tortilla or a piece of bread. But they were offered food all around. Some shouted, "Come get your tortilla!" Others said, "Come! Here is another tortilla with meat!" And still others gave them tamales. In this way, those who had brought nothing to eat were filled.

The pilgrims also carried strong liquor, anise, and sherry. So, if someone sweated too much and wanted to drink cold water, a few drops of liquor were poured into the water to prevent illness. There were anise and sherry for those who went on horseback. Because they could not dismount from the horses, the women and the old tasted the sherry to kill their thirst until they arrived at the water-

ic Chalma aic oniquitoani 'Niaz'." Ihuan inon nocneuh cahuapa oyaya mocuepa huan quilhuia: "Amo xicualantiuh; xitzicuini. Ye yiman timocahuatlaliz. Nehuatl ye ninenentaz." Amoca itech omachiaya tlen quipanoz nocnehuan. Inon cahuapa oyaya omotepexihui ihuan ocalac itzintla cahuayo. Otiquitoque yomopepetoni nozo oquitilizac yolcatl. Amotla oquipano ipampa yehuatl oyac ica nochi iyolo.

Ica ipan in tonaltin omococotzino nonantzin. Tepatique oquito: "Aihmo cehuiz namonantzin. ¡Xiquixtican, xiacan! Aihmo huecahuiz miquiz."

Ihuan amo poliuh ahquen otechilhui: "¡Namechcuamana tepatique! ¡Xicmotenehuilican mahuiztic Tlatihuani Chalma ihuan nanquihtazque quename icihcan mocehuitiz namonantzin!"

Tonochtin tichochoca ihuan oticmotenehuilique Chalma ica Tonantzin Guadalupe. "Tla nanquimocehuilizque —¡Toteotatzin Chalma ihuan Tonantzin Guadalupe!— cecen xihuitl tamechmotlapalhuitihue ica nochi toyolo. Ihuan tonantzin techmecanilitaz. Huel miac tamechtlazohcamachililizque ipampa tetlacolti tihpopolhuizque tonantzin tocahuazque ticnome. ¿Ahquen tequitiz ahquen quimoxotiz piltzitzintin inomequez tziquitzitzin?"

Ihuan Toteotatzin Chalma oquimozcaltili tonantzin. Iqui in que otechmocuepilili tonantzin. Omohuecahuiti monemiti. Ica on xihuitl ihuan occe xihuitl otonyaya tohuentizque ixitlantzinco teotl. Achto zan iqui otiaque: amotla oticuicaque. Ipan ome xihuitl otohuetito ome

ing place. The next watering place was Minas, a small hill. This hill lies above Agua de Cadena.

He who goes to Chalma without a full heart may be in danger on that hill.

We went, my mother and I and two sisters. One of my sisters said, "If I had known that Chalma was so far away, I never would have thought of coming." She was walking, and my other sister who was riding a horse turned around and said, "Don't be angry. Come along. You can ride the horse, and I will walk." No one could imagine then what was going to happen to my sister. The one who was riding fell. She fell under the horse. We were sure that she had been hurt or that the animal had kicked her. But she was not harmed, because she had set out for Chalma with a full heart.

It was around that time that my mother became very ill.

The witch doctor said, "Your mother is never going to get well. Take her away! Go away! She is going to die!"

But someone gave us this advice: "The witch doctor is deceiving you. Cry out to the great Lord of Chalma, and you will see how soon your mother gets well!"

We all wept and cried out to the Lord of Chalma and to Our Mother of Guadalupe. "If you heal our mother, oh Divine Lord of Chalma and Virgin of Guadalupe, we will go visit you every year with all our hearts. And our mother will lead us! We will go to thank you, for it would be a sad thing to lose our mother! Who would work, who would care for the children, for the little ones?"

candelerotin ihuan *cirios*, xochitl, ipampa otimotlazo-
camachililito que otechmozcaltili tonantzin.
Ye titemo icpac Minastepetl. Tonoana queman macuili
tepoztlapoali huatzincopa. Ye tiahue campa ticochizque
itocayoca: Santa Marta. Ompoyon chanequez ye quipia
tlacuali, atlapozonali, tla ca quinequiz tlayiz ihuan quicoaz
pantzin nozo quicuazque in tlaxcali. Ihuan motecatihue.
Chicueyi tlamachotiliztli oacihualoya ompa Santa
Marta; achi huehuecaton in campa titlacuaque. Nochtin
oquinequia acitihue icihcan. Oquinpehuaya cahuatin;
oncuan on tlamachaxihuaz. Otonacia queman chicueyi
tepoztlamachotiloni yohuali. Ihuan tlacatzitzintin tlen
oquinequia quipozonizque tepitzin atlapozon oncuan on
quizque tepilhuan ihuan tecihuauh oquichihuaya tlitl.
¡Achi cualtzin omohtaya! Nepa, nian tlapopoca; nepa,
nian mototonia coconentoton ica cihuame. Noca tlaca
yahue quitemozque atl campa yehuan ye quimati. Occequi
ocontemoaya cuahuitl. Quimatzatzayatzaya ompa cuauhtlatli, inon huahuauhqui cuahuitl, oncuan on amo popo-
caz. Tlacayo ociaohualoya. Oaxihuac, omozohque zoya-
petlame oncuan on necehuiloz. Noca tlaca atlapozonia
ihuan tlatolonia tlaxcali ihuan tlacuali. Zan niman onete-
coya.
Onehualoya queman nahui tlapoali huatzincopa oncuan
on axihuaz Chalma queman chicome tlapoali.
Icuac tzicuini yoyolime iman on nochtin nenencatzitzintin achi netlalolo ic campa cahuatin. Tla nochtlacatl
nimanalo iqui in tzicuinoa queman nian ipan macuili

And Our Divine Father of Chalma returned our mother to us. That is how he gave our mother back to us. She was to live still a long time. And every year, we went on a pilgrimage to visit the God of Chalma. The first time, we took nothing with us. But the next year, we carried two candle sticks and candles and flowers as an offering to thank him for having given life back to our mother.

And then we came down from the hill of Minas which we had left at about five o'clock in the afternoon. And now we went to where we were going to sleep, the place called Santa Marta. The people there had coffee and food ready for those who were thirsty or wanted to buy bread or tortillas. Then the pilgrims were ready to go to sleep.

We arrived at Santa Marta at eight o'clock in the evening, very far from where we had eaten.

All wanted to arrive fast, and all drove their horses hard. Thus, they would arrive all together. We reached Santa Marta at about eight o'clock in the evening. The men wanted to drink a little coffee. So it was that their wives and children made the fires. What a wonderful sight this was! Smoke appeared here and there, and the women and children warmed themselves by the fires. Meanwhile, the men went to get water in places already known to them. Others went to get firewood. They gathered firewood in the hills—dry wood, so it would not smoke. Many of the people were tired. As they arrived, they laid out their palm mats and rested. Meanwhile, the people drank their coffee and heated the tortillas and food. Then they went to sleep.

61

tepoztlamachotiloni ipan otihue ixpan ce xolal quicuitia Santa Mónica. Huan oc tepitzin opanoaloya ipan ce apantli. Ompoyon tlen yocahuaciaque cahuatemo ihuan nenentiuh *hasta* Ocuila.

Zan niman ocalacoaya nenencatzitzintin nochi in otli campa cate ome tzitzime. Tlanonotzaloya quename tlacatl ye oquipiaya icihuauh ihuan ipilhuan. Ihuan cihuatl mate omic inamic. Inin tlacatl oquitlalhui cihuatl cuicaz Chalma. Quenin oyoleque, oyaque. Ihuan ipampa otlatlacoque Toteotatzin oquinmocuepili cuauhtin. Mota quename monahuatequi ihuan itzintla inin cuauhtin pano tepitzin apantli. Nochtlacatl tlenin ohuilaloya quen ihtitzin oquipiaya tlen mitotizque ixpan in cuauhtin. Cequi tlacatl oquicahuaya in cuatlacecahuil. Cequi cihuame ompoyon omitotiaya ihuan occequi oquitequia intzonhuan ihuan oquipiloaya itech cuahuitl. Cequi cihuame oquiciotomaya intzotzoma ihuan oquipiloaya itech cuahuitl. Mitoaya noihqui oquipiloaya itech cuahuitl ixic conetl ica papaltelton. Tla yomitotique ihuan nochi yoquipililoque, iman on occepa nenemi ye motlaza campa axihuaz Chalma. Mitoaya quename ompoyon mocahua ciahuiztli ompa itzintla inin cuauhtin.

Nochtlacatl aihmo ocahuatemoque: otlamelahuaya *hasta* acizque ixitlantzinco Toteotatzin Chalma. Melahuac oacia teopa; amo *siquiera* omocehuiaya Zan niman cahuatemoya ihuan ocalaquia itic teocali campa mahuiztic topixque omochihuiliaya *misa*.

Tlen onentaya aihmo oc acia *misa*. Aihmo huel omote-

Everyone had to get up at about four o'clock in the morning in order to be in Chalma at seven.

When the horses galloped, all of the pilgrims quickened their pace to keep up with the animals. If all the people hurried, there were times that by five o'clock in the morning, we had already gone through a village called Santa Mónica. Quickly we passed over a river there. And those who were weary of riding horseback continued on foot as far as Ocuilan.

Then the pilgrims continued along a path where there grew pines. It was said that one of them had once been a man with a wife and children and that the other was a widow. The man offered to take the widow to Chalma. They got excited and off they went. But because they sinned, Our Divine Father turned them into trees. There they stand, still embracing one another. And from the foot of the trees comes a stream of water. Everyone who journeyed there for the first time was expected to dance in front of these trees. Some of the men used to leave their hats there. Some women danced and some cut off their braids and hung them on the tree. The umbilical cords of babies were also hung in little bags on the trees. When people had danced and hung up their offerings, they set out for Chalma again. It was said that one left all one's weariness under these trees.

After this, men did not dismount from their horses. They went straight on until they had reached the feet of Our Lord of Chalma. When they reached the church, they did

quipachoaya tlican ye tlaca oacique. Cequi cihuame motlaliaya mocehuizque nocauh cequi oyaya tianquizco tlacoazque tlen inon quicuazque tlacotonali. Ihuan omolhuiaya: "Topan otlacactiac; ipampa on aihmo tihcaque *misa*. Ma tocehuican ihuan zan niman tiazque tihmotlapalhuizque tomahuizticteco idios."

Ihqui omochihuaya; onecehuiloya ihuan zan niman ohuilaloya nexopapacoz, niamohuiloz ican atl tlen panotica ca itzintlan teopantli—cuali tiquitozque apantli patlahtic. Canon oyaya maltizque cihuame, tlaca ihuan piltzitzintin—ompoyon omaltiaya.

Ye yiman yomaltique, yotlacuaque nelhuilo: "Yotocehuique; ma ye yiman tiacan ompa itic teocali. Ompa techmochilitoc Tomahuiztatzin."

Zan niman ocalaquia teopa tlen ocuicaya mohuentiquez tlen quimotlacolilizque Toteotatzin onemanaloya ca pochcopa ica tenemac: ahquen cuica ce *cirio*, ahquen cuica *veladoras*, ahquen cuica *aceite* mohuentiquez; ahquen cuica xochitl, xochixaloctin ihuan quicuitia *manteles*, tlen motlalia ipan cuauhtlapechtli in Toteotatzin. Icuac calaquizque nochtinin mahuiztic tlaca topixcatzintli micatz quinmonamiquiliz ica teochihualatl. Oncuan on quinmotlateochihuiliz ica atl.

Omoquixtiaya topixque ica yeyi *acólitos*. Ce ocuicaya in coroz huan ome ocuicaya *cirios* tlatlatihue. Ihuan inomequez mohuentique noihqui ocuicaya *estandarte* de campa techan nozo texolal. Tecana ce cihuatl quimapixtic popochcomitl popocataz ihuan quinmocalaquilia topixque

not even stop to rest. They dismounted and entered the church where the good priest was about to begin the mass.

Those who were on foot did not arrive in time to hear mass. They no longer were in a hurry since they knew they would be late. Some of the women sat down to rest while others went to the market place to buy food for the midday meal. "We were late," they said. "That is why we did not hear mass. First we will rest, and then we will go to greet the Good God."

And so it was; they rested and then they went to wash their heads and feet in the water of a very wide river which runs below the church. It was there that women, men, and children went to bathe.

Having bathed and eaten their meal, they talked among themselves. "We have rested. Let us go to the church where the good father is waiting for us."

Then the pilgrims carried into the church the offerings they had brought to Our Divine Father. In a procession, the people formed two rows to enter the church; some walked on the left and others on the right. Some carried long wax tapers, others vigil lights. One carried the oil (which the pilgrims were to leave for the lamp of the sanctuary). Others carried flowers, vases, and even altar cloths for the altar of Our Divine Father. As they entered, the good priest came to meet them with holy water. And he blessed them with the water. The priest met them with three altar boys. One bore the cross, and the other two carried wax candles. And the pilgrims carried banners

65

itic teocali ihuan nenencatztzintin omoteochihuaya. Zan
niman motlancuaquetza ixpantzinco Toteotatzin. Cequi
ochocaya, cequi omoteochihuaya, occequi quimotlazo-
camachililia tlen ipampa oquimomaquixtili.

Inimequez nenecaltzitzintin nozo mohuentizquez quiz-
aya de in xolal Malacateticpac ipan ome tonali metztli
enero; ihuan oacia Chalma ipan nahui tonali enero. Iman
on mocechuizque ihuan zan huel teopa yezque. Ihuan
niman mitoaya Reyes, iman on omochihuaya ce ilhuitl
mahuiztic ompa Chalma, ica yeyi topixcatzitzintin. Cetzin
motlatoltiz ipan *púrpito* ihuan quinmolhuiliz:

"¡In nenencame ica toteotatzin! ¡Toteotatzin nian ti-
quinmopilia mopilhuantzitzin in huecatlaca! Mitzmote-
potztoquilia. Cualcuauhtehua incal ihuan yoyolime, ipampa mopantzinco oyolehque hualazque mocxitlantzinco.

"Tehuatzin xiquinmaquili ce cuali otli ihuan ce cuali
nemiliztli pipiltzitzintin. Oncuan on tlacayoh monemizque
tatatin yehuan huepahui ihuan noihqui mitzhualmotepotz-
toquilizque. Yenin quitonezqui quimititia otli tepilhuan;
icuac ye huehueyi *cual* ilnamquiquizque. Icuac titziqui-
tzitzin totatzin, tonantzin, otechmohuentilito ompa
Chalma."

Yopanoc inin ilhuitl. Moztlatica neehualo cualcan ah-
quehuantzitzin monequi ixtlamatihuaz ompa Malinalco.
Ompoyon on mocuaya xochicuali quename *lima, granada.*
Noihqui omocoaya achi huelic pantzin. Ihuan ocuicaya
inin xochicuali ica pantzin icuac yehualazque oanazque
oncuan hualhuiloaz techachan. Noihqui tlalcacahua-

which showed the names of thcir villages. In front of them, walked a woman with a smoking incense burner. Then the priest let the pilgrims into the church. They prayed as they walked.

Then all of them knelt at the feet of Our Divine Father. Some wept, others prayed. Still others gave thanks for having been saved from dangers and illnesses.

A beautiful ceremony was held with three priests. One spoke from the pulpit and said to them:

"Pilgrims, you who have arrived in the presence of God! Oh God of ours, behold thy children who have come from afar! They have come to seek thee. They have left their homes and their animals! They have wanted to come to thy feet!

"Be with them on their way and give their children a good way of life! When their parents are gone, these children will grow up and they will come to thee again. This is what we call giving a good example to one's children. When they grow up, they will remember. When we were little, our father and mother took us to give thanks at Chalma!"

The fiesta ended. The next day, those who wanted to see Malinalco got up early. In that village, they bought fruits such as limes and pomegranates and also a very tasty bread. And they took the fruit and the bread for the journey home. They also bought a candy made of peanuts mixed with brown sugar. When they returned to Chalma, they carried all these things into the church. The men

67

panela. Nochi in ocalaquia teopa Chalma. Onemanaloya
tlacatzitzintin ica cihuame ica opochcopa ica teyehman
ihuan tenepantla mopiliaya tlen mopanoltiz topixque
quinmoteochihuiliz huacaltin ican ye tetentoc ica xochicuali Malinalco.

Ye yiman hualoanazque; ye nochtlacatl, tlaca, cihuame
ica pipiltzitzintin huiloa teopa. Zan noihqui motlatoltia
topixque: "¡Ma ce cuali otli namechmaquili in Toteotatzin! Oncuan on ce xihuitl ipan in totazque totlapalozque
ihuan ticmotlapalhuizque inintzin cuauhtechmopilquiti-
toc; topampa omomiquili. Ihuan ma yehuatzin namech-
moteochuilhuili."

Ican cuali tlatoltin motelhuiliaya topixque. Nochtlacatl
chochocoa ihuan quimolhuilia Mahuiztic Teotl ma cuali
otli quinmaquili ihuan tepilhuan ma cuali nemiliztli.
"Oncuan on mocxitlantzinco tipopolahuizque. Zan ye on
huel miac totlatlauhtia."

Ihuan topixque quinmoteochihuilia ica tlateochihualatl.
Achi chochocoa ihuan neteochihualotihuitz. Icuac quixoa
in itic teocali amo necuepalo, zan tzinenemohualotiuh
iman yoquixohuac in itic teocali ma tiquitocan ipan
cementerio. Ye yiman on cuali nenemoa ihuan necahuatla-
lilo. Oncuan on ye huiloaz ipan texolal. Quixoa Chalma
ipan chicnahui tonali *enero.*

Yeco quipanotihuitze nochi otli tlen achto quipanoque.
In Minas tlacuazque. Ompoyon nochtin que icohuiloac
noihqui tlacualo, atlihua ihuan quimatlitia cahuatin.
Oncuan on quixicozque acizque Ajusco. Cequi tlacatl

68

stood in a line on the left and the women on the right. The priest walked between them, blessing the wooden crates of the food from Malinalco.

Now everyone was ready to leave Chalma. All the people—men, women, and children—went to the church, and the priest spoke again. "May Our Divine Father be with you on your way! May we meet again on this day a year from now! May we greet each other again and visit the Lord who is crucified on the cross, He who died for us! May He bless you all!"

With these good words the priest said farewell to all. The pilgrims wept and begged the good God to be with them on the road and to give their children a good way of life. "We will return," they cried. "And we will kneel at thy feet again. That is what we pray thee, nothing more!"

Then the priest blessed them with holy water while everyone wept great tears and left the church praying. On leaving the church, they did not turn their faces from the Lord of Chalma but walked backwards until they had passed the chapel of the cemetery. Then they turned faces frontwards and mounted their horses. Thus, they set out for their villages again. They left Chalma on the ninth of January.

They returned by the same road they had already travelled. They had breakfast at Minas. All the pilgrims ate there, drank water, and fed the horses so they would not have to eat again until Ajusco. Some slept in Ajusco, and others rested in Topilejo. It was there that the new *mayor-*

cochia Ajusco ihuan occequi oacia Tupilejo. Ompoyon onecalotiloya. Zan niman *mayordomo* yencuic Milpa Alta quipia tlen quitetlamacaz nochtin nenencatzitzintin mohuentiquez. Ompoyon tetzatzatzililo. Tlen inomequez ocochque Ajusco yeyeco queman chicome tlapoaliztli huatzincopa. Quimetetequetza yeyi nozo nahui tlaca; oncuan on ahuel panozque mohuentiquez queniman yotlacuaque ma tiquitocan almazalolo. In *mayordomo* yencuic yehuatl on techiaz Tupilejo. Quitemaca tamali, tlaxcali, *arroz*, tlimoli, yetl. Tlatlanihua: "¿Quezqui tlacatl tiquinmiquilitz? ¿Nozo motlauhtzinco huitze? Oncuan on ma mitzmaquilican achi hueyi tlacuali, miac tamali ihuan miac tlaxcali. Tla aca huitz quinequi ineuhtli ma mamopacho, ma quitlani."

Ye yiman ye ticalaquizque matlactli tonali *enero* tlatzilini San Pablo Oztotepec, tlatzilini San Pedro Actopan. Inon quitoznequi ye huitze mohuentiquez. Zan niman pehua tlatzilini ompa Momochco Malacateticpac, oncuan on ye cate tlatzotzonquez ipan otli can quicuitia Tlalatlahco noca mohuentiquez mocehuitoque San Pedro Actopan. Quitlacali yeyi tlacueponaltin oncuan San Pedro.

Ye yiman on inomequez tlatzotzona yahue techiazque; icuac tiquita ye hualcoxoni *gente* icpac tepetl San Pedro. Ye yiman on tlatzotzona. Ihuan tlen nenenquez quimamati huitze Totatzin Chalma. Quimonamiquilizque ica popochtli, ica *cirios* tlatlatazque, ompa Santa Marta teocaltzintli, ompoyon nochipa cecen xihuitl, ompoyon omoquixtiaya, ompoyon omocalaquiaya nenenquez.

domo of Milpa Alta had to give food to all the pilgrims on their return. He had to meet them there in Topilejo. Those who had slept in Ajusco arrived at about seven o'clock in the morning. Three or four men from Milpa Alta came out to meet them.

They stopped the pilgrims to give them breakfast there.

The new mayordomo had to wait in Topilejo. He gave the pilgrims tamales, tortillas, rice, black mole, and beans. And the mayordomo would ask, "How many people have you brought with you? How many people are with you? Let them be given plenty of food, plenty of tamales and plenty of tortillas. If anyone wishes to drink pulque, let him come forth and ask for it."

At dawn, on the tenth of January, the bells began to ring in San Pablo Oztotepec. Then they were rung in San Pedro Atocpan. This meant that the pilgrims were about to arrive. Then the bells of the town Milpa Alta begin to peal, telling the musicians to be ready, to wait on the road called Tlalatlahco, while the pilgrims rested in San Pedro Atocpan. At San Pedro three fire rockets were lighted, and they burst in the air.

By this time, the musicians were waiting. Suddenly there came the crowd of pilgrims, down from the slopes of San Pedro. The band began to play. And here came the pilgrims, carrying a banner with Our Dear Father of Chalma! With incense and flaming wax candles, they were received inside the church of Santa Marta, which the pilgrims leave and return to year after year.

Ic oncuan Milpa Alta omotiaya occequi mohuentiquez. Hualehua ica ompa huehcatlaltin, quename Ameca, tlazcaltecaz, Puebla ihuan chalca. Nochtin on ica ompa opanoaya cecen xihuitl icuac oyaya noihqui quimotlapalhuizque mahuiztic teotl Chalma. Opanoya cequi metztli *febrero* occequi metztli *mayo* ihuan occequi opanoaloya ipan metztli *agosto* ipan cempuali ihuan chicueyi. Ontlalhuiquixtiaya ompa Chalma. Ihuan tlen *septiembre* oyaya otlalhuiquixtiaya ilhuitl San Miguel.

Nochin nenencatzitzintin omopanoltiaya ica tianquizco Momochco ca yixpan *juzgado* ihuan omotlecahuiaya nochi tepetl itoca Tepeticpac. Ohuilaloya panoaz can metztaya ce coroz de tetl itocayoca Tzitzintitla. Axcan aihmo metztica in coroz de tetl ipampa oquichihque caltin tlaca cuacuali ihuan ica on tetexcaltin oquincuecuepotzque. Oncuan on oquiz tetl, ica on ica omochihchique caltin. Zan niman oyaya ica Buenavista otli. Oacia campa ca amatomatl ihuan ye ompoyon omomanaya nochtlacatl; oncuan on onquinchiaya inomequez nenencame, onecahualo tlacuitlapa. Ye yiman oquititlania ce tlacatl tlatlaniz tla ye nochtlacatl yonecentlalilo. Oncuan on ye tlamach oanaloz. Noihqui omopanoltiaya San Pablo, San Salvador, Tupilejo ihuan ica Ajusco. Oquipiaya tlen panoaz nochi otli, tlen nenencame Milpa Alta opanoque.

Tlazcaltecaz cequi otlatoaya macehualcopa, cequi caxtilancopa. Noihqui chalca otlatoaya macehualcopa. Amequeñoz noihqui tlatoaya macehualcopa quename tehuan titlatoa.

72

Besides our own pilgrims, others were to be seen passing through Milpa Alta. They came from distant places such as Amecameca, Tlaxcala, Puebla, and Chalco. All of them came through the village, year after year, on their way to visit the good God of Chalma. Some passed in the month of February, others in May, and still others in the month of August—on the twenty-eighth of August. They went to celebrate their village saints in Chalma. Those who passed through in September went to honor Saint Michael.

All the pilgrims passed through the square in front of the courthouse and went up a hill called Tepeticpac. They went by some rocks called Tzitzintitla where stood a cross of stone. Today this stone cross is no longer there because people blew up the rocks to build houses on that site. From there came the stone with which they built the houses. Then they went along a street called Buenavista. And then they reached the place of the mulberry tree where everyone gathered. Thus they waited for the pilgrims who had remained behind. And one man was directed to see if all were reunited. Then all of them set out on the road to Chalma, through San Pablo, San Salvador, Topilejo and Ajusco, along the same route followed by the pilgrims of Milpa Alta.

Some of the Tlaxcallans spoke Nahuatl, others Spanish. The people of Chalco also spoke Nahuatl, and those of Amecameca spoke Nahuatl just as we speak it.

73

Inintzin Santa Marta totlazomahuiznantzin. Icuac amo oquimomisatiliaya ilhuitzin, oquimocacahuiliaya yeyecacoa. Ihuan tlacuali otlalhuiquizaya iman on quiahuia nian amo tlapetlania, nian amo otlacuacualacaya.

Ihuan oquizaya mitotiquez. Inimequez mitotiquez quincuitiaya "Santiagome," "Atzcame" ihuan *Danzas.* Iqui in cuali otlalhuiquizaya. Ica teotlac ometequetzaya ce cuahuitl, queman chicueyi tlamachotiloni, teotlac acan quicuecuepotzazque telpocame ica miac tlacuecueponaltin. Inimequez telpocame miactin—ma tiquitocan—nochtin tlen ipan barrio Santa Marta, nochi telpocame ohuehuetzia ica tomin, oncuan on cuali quixtlahuazque. Inin cuahuitl oquicuitiaya *castillo.* Campa nochi tlen

74

IX. SANTA MARTA AND THE DAY OF THE DEAD

Seven are the barrios of Milpa: Santa Marta, San Mateo, La Concha, Santa Cruz, Los Angeles, La Luz, and Guadalupe. The small chapel of Santa Marta draws hundreds of villagers to attend her feast on July 29. But far more important is the Feast of the Dead. During the night between November 1 and 2 the head of each household of Milpa Alta is proud of his ofrenda—a table set up with stews, candles, breads, liquor, glasses of water, candles, and cigarettes for the Faithful Departed. All night the members of the family accompany the "little dead ones," the beloved ancestors who have come to spend this one night of the year among the living. But first comes the day of Santa Marta.

The Virgin Santa Marta was Our Beloved Mother. When a mass was not offered on her feast day, she sent down snakes of water. When her feast day went well, then there were no frightful rain storms or lightning nor did it thunder.

At her fiesta, the dancers appeared, the *Santiagos*, the *Atzcame*, and the *Danzas*. With these the fiesta was a success. A pole was set up at about eight o'clock at night and the firecrackers attached to it were exploded by boys. These boys, all from the quarter of Santa Marta, saved their money and co-operated in order to pay for all these things. This pole was known as *El Castillo*. All the men, women, and children from around Santa Marta came to

oquimehualhuiaya Santa Marta, nochi on tlaca cihuame huan pipiltzitzintin ohualhuilaloya tlachaloz, icuac opehuaya tlacuecuepotzaya in *castillo*. Nochipa nozo cecenxihuitl oquitliquechiaya queman matlactli ihuan ce tlapoali tepoztlamachotiloni yohuali.

Oquipiaya hornotin techachan. Oncuan on ica oquichihuaya pantzin ihuan oquincuitiaya pancuitlaxtli. Yehua on nochipa omochihuaya. Noihqui oacia micailhuitl oquichihuaya *bizcochos* huan *tortas*, inon pantzin poyec. Ihuan cequi quicuitiaya *goyetes*; icuaticpac oquitlaliliaya in *azúcar*. Yehuatl on quinamacazque ipan tianquiztli ihuan nochtin occequi *barrios* quicuaya ica quichazque micatzitzintin. Noihqui ipan in *barrio* cequi tlaca otlachiquia oncuan on onyez neuhtli quemanian oyeya hasta oncuan monamacaz. Nochipa otlachicoya ipampa amo oyeya atzintli; oyaya *pero* zan tepitzin. Zan ica neiceliloz ihuan *para* tlacuali noihqui. Ihuan neuhtli icotemoya tlacuali quename axan toconi ce *refresco*. Inimequez tlaca cualcan yomocuepato in cuentla ica necuatl. Huitze almazaloa nozo tlayi. Huan oyaya zan niman tequitizque. Cequi oquinenemitiaya *yunta* ica cahuatin. Omitiaya "Yahue tlapehuazque."

Ihuan ocualicaya pantzin oncuan Xochimilco ihuan San Gregorio Atlapulco, ce chicueyi tonali ohualatlanamacaya. Zan onepapatlaloya; cequi hualaya *domingo* tlanamacazque, *lunes*, *martes* ihuan *miércoles*. Occequi tlacatl tlacuali oyeya tianquiztli icihcan omocuepaya ompa ipan in xolal Momochco Malacateticpac.

enjoy themselves when the Castillo began to explode. It was lighted every year at about eleven o'clock at night.

The people of Santa Marta had ovens in their homes. In these ovens, they baked bread—a bread called "leather bread." They worked at this every day. Then came the Feast of the Dead, and they made pastry, buns, salted breads, and others called *goyetes*, sprinkled with sugar. All of this they sold in the market place, and the people of the other quarters bought it for the Vigil of the Souls. Some of the men of this ward worked the maguey plants to make pulque which they sold from time to time in the market place. They worked the maguey plants every day because there was very little water. There was water only for washing and cooking. Pulque was drunk to help the food go down—just as we drink soda pop today. The men went out to the fields and returned with the sweet water of the maguey plants. They came back for breakfast and then returned to their work. Some plowed with horses.

The bread baked in Santa Marta they also took to Xochimilco and San Gregorio Atlapulco. They went to sell every week in these places. The people took turns. Some went to sell on Sundays, others on Monday, Tuesday, or Wednesday. They would return on that same day to the lands of Milpa Alta.

In those days, none of the people knew their way to Mexico City. They knew only the towns of Xochimilco and San Gregorio Atlapulco.

77

Yiman on amo huel ca oquixmatia hualaz Mexico; zan huel ye Xochimilco ihuan San Gregorio. Noihqui oyaya cuauhtla cuacuahuizque; oquitetemaya cuahuitl. Oncuan on tla quiauhtaz *agosto* ihuan *septiembre* yehuan yoquitepetlaliaya incuauh. Tlen quinequizque ica quihuixitizque in pantzin. Iqui in ic onemia tlatihuanime ihuan cihuatzitzintin Santa Marta.

Achtocopa in nenonotzaloya icuac tocoltzitzihuan, mach oyeya ce telpocatl tlatcihque huan itahtzin yomomiquili. Huan nantzintli oquichoquilitemia itelpoch ica otlica pampa oquizaya. Pampa zan niman tlathui, mehua zan yahui tlan imaicnehuan ca otlica, in huinti ca pahtli, in huinti ca neuhtli. Ihuan ayic oquihtoaya "Ye huitz micailhuitl. Tlen ticcihuazque, nonantzin?" Ayic tlon quihtoaya.

Ye yiman oacico micailhuitl huan nantli quilhuia "Notelpoch, amo ticmati tlen ye topan huitz? Tla xiquitani, tla nemizquía motahtzin, axcan ye ohualtlatentazquia. Ye oticohuani inon ca netlahuililo quicuitia in candelatin, tehuatl amotla mitztequipachoa. Cuali yez ticnemiliz cana timomaihtoti, ic ompa titequitiz ica xicoa ce candela, in popochtli ihuan in papanton, ticmochialtilizque motahtzin huan mocoltzitzihuan.

Quihto telpocatl "Amo monantzin. Ahquen yomic yomic. Acmo mayana, acmo amiqui, acmotla quilehuia. Nechnamiqui. Achi hueyi namiqui pampa oniquic hueyi neuhtli huan hueyi pahtli."

Zan niman inin tlatzicaconetl oyac in huintito occepa

The people of Santa Marta also went to the woods to gather firewood and fell trees.

If it happened to rain in August or September, they would have—by that time—their firewood, dry and ready to bake the bread. So lived the men and women of Santa Marta.

Thus passed this feast. But before we knew it, the people of the village were already preparing for the Day of the Dead. How well I remember the bonfires in front of each house and the thousands of marigolds—flowers of the dead.

In olden times, when our grandparents were still alive, a story was told about a lazy youth whose father had died. His mother went about the streets weeping for the boy whenever he left the house. By early morning he was up to go off with his friends in to the streets to get drunk on strong liquor or pulque. He never said, "The Day of the Dead is coming. What shall we prepare for the dead, mother?" He never talked about these things.

Then came the Day of the Dead. "My son," his mother said, "do you realize what is coming upon us? If you had known your father, if he had lived longer, he would now be given something to eat. We would have bought candles for him. But you never take anything seriously. It would be good if you could get a job and work so you could buy a wax candle, an incense burner, and bread to welcome your father and grandfather."

"No, mother," answered the boy, "he who is dead is

79

itlan imaicnehuan ihuan zan huitlatica huiptlatica yacitica in micailhuitl. Anquilhuia nantli "Tlen mopan mochihua? Amo tocaqui tlen nimitzilhuia? Xitetemoti in cuahuitl, ica tetoniquizque, nenonotzaloyan in mocoltzitzihuan. Ca huitze micatzitzintin huan cececoa, pampa nochi yohuali nenenemoa. Ca in hyehuantin ilhuicac ic motepilia. Ipampa onninicnequizquia timotequipachoz tepitzin. Motahtzin hualaz huan amotla ticpia tlen ticmacazque. Nehuatl tiquita, ahueli nitequiti. Amonca canin titequitiz."

Quihtoa piltontli "Amo ximotequipacho tinonana. Amo ticpia cachi cuali candela. Nehua niaz cualcan nicmitiuh ocotl huan tictlalizque huey ocotl ipan caltemitl."

Zan niman quihto nantli "Ma telhuan cuahuitl."

Oyac piltontli huan zan niman ipan oteotlaquiz. Cuauhtla omixpolo. Nantzintli quitemoa ipiltzin, chocatinemi ica pan otli. Nian micailhuitl. Nohuian nacatamalolo. Tlacuachihualo. Ca techialo micatzitzintin. Ahuiac caltin ipampa tlapopochhuilo ihuan tlanextililo ca candelatin. Huan inin cihuatl chocatinemi. Amo quinextia itelpoch. Niman oquito "Tlen ipan mochihua nopiltzin?"

Ihuan omonacacicatecac huan oquicaque micatzitzintin motlatlahtoltique. "Xitlatlachia. Xictemo motelpoch. Tleca ic ihqui on ticahuilizcahua? Tleca ticacahua? Amo tictzatzilia. Ipampa on tinantli. Ticmitequiz. Ticnacazhuilanaz. Oncuanon mitzneltocaz. Tlen axan xitlacoya. Ca ca moconeuh?"

"Xictemoti, ipan cuauhtlatli ilpiticac, pampa tlacihque.

dead. He is not hungry anymore. He is not thirsty. He needs nothing. But I am thirsty, thirstier than they are, because I drank a lot of pulque and liquor last night."

Then the idle one went off with his friends to get drunk. And the Feast of the Dead was only three days away.

"What is wrong with you?" said his mother. "What is the matter with you? Why won't you listen to me? Go out and get some firewood to give warmth to your grandparents. The beloved, the little dead ones—they are on their way. Those who live in the heavens are trembling with cold. How I wish you would pay attention to these things! Your father will come and we will have nothing to offer him. You know I cannot work; there is no work for me anywhere."

"Don't worry, mother," said the youth. "We may not have the best wax candles but I will go early to gather pine branches and we will place them in a bonfire at the door of the house."

"Let it be good firewood," said the mother.

The boy went away and night fell upon him in the woods. He got lost. The mother seeks her son. She goes about weeping in the streets. The Feast of the Dead has come. Tamales are being made everywhere; food is prepared—all to await the return of the beloved dead. Everywhere the homes are smoking with incense and lighted with wax candles. And the woman goes about crying. She cannot find her son. Then she says, "What has happened to my boy?"

Otiquilhuiaya quitemotin in cuamitl ica tiempo huan yehuatl amo oquinec. Nian candela quicuaz. Omitznanquili quicuitin ocotl ca techtlanextiliz. Inin oticualilpitiquizque. Xiauh pan cuahtlatli, aca xitlatlauhti ma mitzhuica, ma mitzyolaliti. Ihuan ticnextitin motelpoch can otiquilpique, ca ce zacamecatl ilpitica itech ce cuauhtzontetl. Huan otechitac tihualpanotaque huan iman on yomomauhti. Ihuan quihto "Notahtzin, nonantzin! Ye ipan nonantzin onechmahuizquia huan onechahuaya nitequitiz. Nehuatl amo nicnec onitequit. Notlatlacol mochihua iquin nihtica."

Oquittac icihtzin, yohpacihtzin, iyexpacihtzin, yicnehuan ihuan itahtzin quitlahpalotiquizqueh. Quihtocayotia "Tlen oncuan tai?" "Oncan nechca hasta cuac namocueptzinotihueh, in amocalaquizqueh ilhuicac ihtic. Ye iman on anechmotohtomitehuazqueh nian. Mah nian amechmochili."

Zan niman oyac, ohuiloac nochtin micatzitzintin. Oncan quintechichilo. Ocalacoahqueh inon, icuac cente yehui ilhuitl canah, tlathuiquixtiz, quimama iquimil, quimama ce ayatontli, quimama ce petlatontli. Ca netecoz can tepan tlayohuaz.

Huan inin piltontli ompo quion oquilpitiquizqueh. Yoacic nantli. Otlehcoc cuauhtlatli ca ce tlacatzintli. Ca huehca. Huan amo oquinexti itelpoch. Ohuala tlaocoya cihuatl amo quinixti itelpoch. Zan niman ohuala ipan ichan huan choca.

Ye niman micatzitzintin tlacayo, quimoresponsotilia,

She went to bed and lay on her side. And then she heard the loved ones, the dead, speaking. "Go out and look for your son. Why have you abandoned him? Why have you left him? You do not scold him, though you are his mother. You should beat him! You should pull him by the ears! Meanwhile you will have to be sad.

"Where is your son? Go out and seek him. He is tied up in the woods because of his laziness. We had already warned him to go out and get firewood but he did not want to. He refused to buy candles. He answered that he would go get pine wood to light our way. Now he is wretched because we have tied him up. Go to the woods. Get someone to take you there and help you along the way. You will find your son bound to the trunk of a tree. He saw us coming toward him and he was filled with terror. He yelled 'Father! Mother! My mother would have loved me if I had gone to work. But I did not want to work; it is my fault that I am here!' "

This boy saw his grandmother, his great grandmother, his great-great grandmother, his dead brothers and sisters, his father—all of whom came to greet him. "What are you doing there?" they asked. "I have been left here until you go away again, until you return to heaven. It will not be until then that you will come back to untie me. I will await you here."

Then the little dead ones all continued on their way to their homes, where they were expected.

They make their way into the village where things have

83

neteochihualoh tepampa, canin ca ye teyemic. Zan niman ohuiloac cihuatl, omotecac cochi yohualtica. Huan icuac otlathuic, oquitac itelpoch yocalaquico. Quilhuia "Can otoyeya tlacihque?"

Huan piltontli choca. Mamamacuecuepotza, tzahtzi quen coyotl huan quilhuia inantzin "Melahuac, axcan quema nonantzin. Ye noneltocac que melahuac huitzeh micatzitzintin."

been prepared for them. Each one carries his load; each one carries a bundle on his tumpline; each one carries a little mat where he is to sleep when night falls.

So it was that the boy was bound there. The mother went to the distant woods accompanied by a man, but she could not find her son. Sadly she returned to her house and wept.

But by this time the little dead ones have arrived in the village. Men and women sing for them. People pray for them. Now, all the people of the town have received their dead at home.

Then the woman went to sleep in her house. At dawn she saw her son back home. She said, "Where were you, lazy one?"

But the boy cries. He wrings his hands until the bones crack. He howls like a coyote. "You were right," he tells his mother. "Now I believe that the dead *do* come back."

Inin *barrio* itoca Santa Cruz. Noihqui otlachiquia ica necuatl quename Santa Marta. Oquipiaya necuatl oncuan mocuepa neuhtli.

Inimequez *barrio* oquipiaya ce nemiliztli ipantzinco Toteotatzin. Tlanonotzalo quename icuac aciz ilhuitzin Santa Cruz mohtaz tlilcuiz quename icuac xotla ce cali. Ihuan ahquen oquitaya iqui on quipiaya tlen quimachotiz ihuan queman tlacoyohuali quitatiuh campa ca tlamachotili. Amo timatizque cox melahuac, cox amo melahuac, tlen otechnonotzaya: quename inintzin Toteotatzin omotenextiliaya tomin. Iqui in ica aca omocuepaya tlatquihua. Iqui in otlanonotzaloya quename zan quimotzatzililizque nozo quimotenehuilizque yehuatzin, Santa Cruz, quimomaquiliz tlen quinequi.

X. MOSLEMS AND CHRISTIANS

The chapel of another quarter of Milpa Alta is dedicated to the Holy Cross. The people also celebrate their yearly fiesta and present dance dramas dating back to the Middle Ages. These were brought to Mexico by the Spanish conquerors and form part of Milpa Alta's European heritage.

Another quarter of Milpa Alta was called Santa Cruz; the people there, like those of Santa Marta, extracted aguamiel to make pulque.

The people of this ward believed it had been favored in a special way by Our God. They said that on the day of the feast of the Holy Cross, one could see a light as big as a house. Whoever saw it had to mark the spot with a stake and return at midnight to find his mark. We do not know whether it is true or not, but it was said that this miraculous light showed where treasure was hidden. In this way, some became rich. They said that by simply crying out the name of the Holy Cross, it gave them all they wanted.

The feast of the Holy Cross was celebrated with candles and processional candle holders. The wax candles were ar-

Noihqui oquimotlalhuiquixtiliaya Santa Cruz ica ciriotin; ica cirialestin motlaehualhuiz in *Santísimo*.

Iquin omochihuaya ipampa amo quiahuia; omoquixtiaya Toteotatzin; mehualhuiaya nochi in xolal. Quemanian otitlaehualoaya ihuan otechacia quiahuitl. ¡Tlen paquiliztli omopiaya tlaca ipampa yoquiauh! Ihuan omitoaya, "Cuentlatin ye huahuaqui—tlaolmitin, yemiltin—nochtin yeco amiqui. Ye tetlacolti que ica cate tocuentlahuan."

Ihuan icuac omotlaehualhuiaya Toteotatzin ihuan topixcatzintli, cano acia *esquina*, ompoyon omocehuitzinoaya in *Santísimo*. Ihuan topixcatzintli omoteochiuhtzinoaya ihuan omotlateochihuiliaya. Iqui in omochihuiliaya ipan nahui *esquina de* in xolal. ¡Coza noihqui mahuizticatzintli in Toteotatzin!

Icuac ilhuitzin *quizá* mitotiquez pastoratin, santiagome ihuan quemanian azcatzitzintin.

Inin pastoratin intzotzoma nochi iztac; oquicuaticpanoaya ce *corona* quename inon *azahares de naranja*. Inin *azahares* oquichichihuaya ica *cera* oquinmacuiaya intzotzoma iztac ihuan ce *arco* omototonpoxhuaya ihuan oquitlaliliaya amaxochitl, oncuan on achi *cual* neciz. Huan tlatzotzonque oquitzotzonaya ce *guitarra* huan ce tlapitzalcuahuitl. Ica on cocone yoquixmatia tlen tlen quitotizque: cana ome metztli omomachtiaya cecen chicueyi tonali *sábado* huan *domingo*. Oncuan on cuali quizalozque tlen mocuicatizque. Huan oquitoaya:

ranged to form an arch around the Most Holy Sacrament.

And when a drought came, Our God, in the Eucharist, was carried around the entire village. Sometimes, when we were walking along in the procession, it started to rain. How happy we were! People had said, "Our fields—our fields of corn and beans—they are dying of thirst! Everything is drying up. Our fields bring us nothing but misery."

So it was that Our Lord was taken by the priest in a procession around the village. At each street corner, the Holy Sacrament was allowed to rest, and the priest prayed and sprinkled the ground with holy water. This was done in all the four corners of the quarter. Our God is a glorious God!

On the days of the feast of the Holy Cross, the shepherdesses danced, as did the Santiagos and the Azcatzitzintin, the little ants.

The shepherdesses wore white dresses and on their heads they wore crowns with orange blossoms made of wax. They were dressed in white and wore fluffy bows and paper flowers and they always looked their best. The musicians played guitars and flutes. The little girls danced well, for they had been practicing for two months, every week on Saturdays and Sundays. They had learned their song well:

> Come: let us go to dance
> In the stable at Bethlehem!

89

Tiahue, tiahue titotizque
ompa *portal* in Belén.
¡Timotilizque Toteotatzin
omotlacatili ompa Belén!

Inimequez cihuantoton ocuicaya ce pipiltontli oquitla-
quentiaya itzotzoma quename Totatzin San Miguel. Inin
pipiltontli amotla omocuicatiaya; zan huel ye oquipiaya
tlen mitotiz intzalan pastoratin. Itzotzoma oquihuicaya
noihqui icorona ihuan ye huitzhuan quename Totatzin
San Miguel. Inimequez cocone oquipiaya tlen mitotizque
nochi in cemilhuitl. Icuac ilhuitzin Toteotatzin oyaya
mocuicatizque nahui *hora* huatzinco ica in candelahuan;
zan niman omitotiaya. Queman chicueyi tlamachotiloni
huatzincopa oquinhuicaya tlaizque ichan *mayordomo*
izoltic. Ihuan nima tlayotlaique occepa oyaya ompa teopa;
occepa mitotia. Noca pehua *misa*, inon moteochiuhtzinoa
yeyi totopixquez ixpantzinco teotl.

Otlatzonquizaya ihuan oyeya tlacuazque ichan *mayordomo* yencuic. Occepa omocuepaya ompa teopa; occepa
mitotia. Yeyi tonali quipia tlen mitotizque. Ipan nahui
tonali huitz *coronación* campa *mayordomo* izoltic ihuan
yencuic oquipiaya tlen motlancuaquetzazque ixpantzinco
Toteotatzin. Ihuan nian cente teteachcan ye quipiaya
cuahxicali ica coronatin. Topixcatzintli oquimotlaliliaya
icuacticpac *mayordomo* izoltic. Achi cuacuali xochitl
ocuicaya in *corona*. Ihuan *mayordomo* yencuic quipiaya
tlen quitlalizque ce *corona* tzotzopiyo. Neci inon *corona* in

90

Let us go visit God
Who has just been born in Bethlehem!

These girls danced around a little boy who was dressed like Our Father Saint Michael. This child did not sing. He only danced among the little shepherdesses. He wore a robe, a crown, and wings just like those of the image of Our Father Saint Michael in the church. The little girls had to dance all day. When the feast of Our Lord came, they picked up their candles and carried them to the church at four o'clock in the morning. There they sang, there they danced. At about eight o'clock in the morning all the children were taken to have breakfast at the home of the out-going mayordomo. Once they had eaten breakfast, the girls returned to the church to dance. Once again, they danced. Then the mass began. It was said by three priests, there, in the presence of God.

The band played again, and the girls went to have their midday meal at the home of the new mayordomo. Then they returned to the church to dance—to dance for three days.

On the fourth day came the coronation of the mayordomos. Both the old and the new mayordomos had to kneel before Our God. An elder, the sexton, held ready in his hands a wooden gourd and two crowns. The priest crowned the old mayordomo with a beautiful wreath of flowers. And to the new mayordomo he gave a crown of thorns—like the one which was placed upon the head of

oquimotlalilique in Toteotatzin. Ihuan topixque iman yoquimotlalili coronatin quinmoteochihuilia ica tlateochihualatl.

Noihqui omitotiaya Santiagome. Inimequez itlaquen oyeya ce *capote* chichiltic, in cuatlacecahuitl de tepoztli ica icahhuan ihuan mediastin. *Cristianos* ocuicaya ce *estandarte* ica ce coroz ihuan *mahometanos* quihuicatze ce pantli ihuan zan huel ye otlatoaya ipampa Mahoma. Ihuan ohcan omoxeloaya. Cequintin oquimilhuiaya mahometanos ihuan occequi *cristianos*. Icuac opehuaya momaga ican *machetes*, omolhuiaya,

> ¿Campa ca morreino?
> ¡Mahoma achi tlamacani!—mitoaya
> Xiquita tehuan ticristianos,—tlatoa in *cristiano*—,
>   ihuan amo
> Toteotatzin amo tlamacani quename Mahoma.
> —Ihuan oquitentiaya machetetin ipan tlalticpatli

Santiagome noihqui omitotiaya yeyi tonali ihuan omomagaya. Quenon mitoa caxtilancopa "omodesafiaroa" nozo omotlatlatoltiaya. Iman omotlatlatoltiaya cente quitoa.

Xinechitititi: ¿Campa ca morreino? ¿Campa motlanequiliz?

Nianca cate *mahometanos* achi mitztlanizque ica nochi mocristiandad.

Ihuan zan niman omomagaya ica espadatin. Iquin

Our Lord. Once they had been crowned, the priest blessed them with holy water.

And the Santiagos danced. They wore red mantles, metal helmets, shoes and hose. The Christians carried a banner with a cross on top and the Moslems another flag. They yelled a great deal about Mohammed. The groups were divided in two. Some were called Mohammedans and the others Christians. When they began to fight with their swords, they yelled:

"Where is your might?"

"Mohammed hits hard!"

"Look out, for we are Christians, and Our Lord God does not strike in the same way as does Mohammed!" And they pounded the floor with their swords.

The Santiagos danced for three days and fought fiercely. As we say in Spanish, they "challenged one another," and they yelled at one another. In their challenges they cried out, "Show me! Where is your might? What went wrong with your plans?"

"The Moslems are about to finish off all Christendom!"

Then they struck at one another with their swords. They danced. When the Christians won and the Mohammedans lost, Mohammed fell upon the ground and died. Then the bells of the church tolled and the band played mournful music. And Mohammed began to weep.

"Where is my head?" he cried out. "I never knew that the Christians would destroy me like this!"

omitotiaya. Ihcuac otlalania *cristianos* ihuan Mahoma otlapoloaya ohuetzia ipan tlalticpactli. Oaquetztaya ihuan omiquia. Opehuaya in tepoztlatzilinaltin otzilinia ihuan tlatzotzonquez noihqui oquitzotzonaya coza tetlacolti. Tlen oquitoaya inin Mahoma opehuaya *choca* ihuan quitoaya: "¿Campa oyeya notzonteco? ¡Amo onihmatiaya quename nechtlanizque *cristianos!*"

Ihuan icuac necoronaroz in yencuic *mayordomo* ahquen tlalhuiquixtiz ce xihuitl.

Can onichantiaya itoca *barrio* San Mateo campa metztoc hueyi teotl ahquen quimoxotilia tobarrio. Yehuatzin coza cualtzin intlac chantlaca ihuan chantlaca coza oquimotlazotiliaya noihqui.

Icuac oacia tonali iilhuitzin omochihuaya ilhuitl cuali. Oquizaya *procesión* ica otlica. Chantlaca oquitoaya: "¡Ma onye *procesión!* Oncuan on toteotatzin motlateochihuiliz otli. Oncuan aic tlatechpanoz."

Huan amo quimotlailhuiquixtilizque, iman on omotemaguiliaya ica cetl. Ihuan ohuaquia miltin. Ica on chantlaca omomanaya: cequi tetlaitizque, cequi tetlamacazque, occequi tecenamacazque ihuan occequi castillopa. Occequintin mohuentia *cohetes*.

Huitzi de San Lorenzo, Santa Marta, Santa Cruz ihuan La Concha. Nochtin on huitzi ica ceratin, ica popochtli ihuan *cohetes*. Tlatzonquiza *misa* topixcatzintli ihuan quinmonamiquiliz in *salveros*.

Ipan metztli *diciembre* mitoa *nochibuena* achi cualtzin omochihuaya. Amo oyeya techan motlacatiliz toteotatzin

94

It was at this time that the new mayordomo—who was to hold office for one year—was crowned.

My home was in the quarter of San Mateo, where stands in his chapel the image of the great saint who watches over our part of the village.

He is good to the people, and the men and women of the quarter love him with a strong love.

When the day of his fiesta came, it was celebrated in the most wonderful way. The procession came out through the streets. "Let the procession come out!" said the people. "Thus our great saint will bless the streets! No harm can come upon us—ever!"

And when his feast day was not celebrated, then he would scourge us with frost, and our cornfields withered.

All the people of the district joined together for the fiesta. Some paid for the breakfast, some gave the midday meal, and others gave the supper. Still others gave the castillos of fireworks. And some brought firecrackers as an offering to San Mateo.

People came from San Lorenzo, Santa Marta, Santa Cruz, and La Concha. All came with candles, incense, and fireworks. When the priest had sung the mass, the *salveros* —officials of the districts—took their own images of the Child to the main door of the church. With a ceremonial cross and surrounded by candles, the priest came out to meet the images of the Child Jesus in order to place them on the high altar. So it was that the seven images from the seven wards were placed in the church. Then the band

sino cada barrio oquihuicaya ce teotatzin ihuan ixpan *puerta principal* teopa. Ica coroz *alta* huan *ciriales* oquinmonaniquiliaya topixque can oc in oquinmotlaliliaya *altar mayor.* Ompoyon ometztaya nochi de tlen chicome *barrio* huan otlatzotzonaya *música.* Icuac quinmocalaquiliaya teopa achi cualtzin oyeya. Achi miac *cohetes* omotlacalia. Oyeya xochitl.

Iqui in oyeya *nochibuena*; cualtzin oquizaya teopa ilhuitl.

started playing. It was a wonderful thing to see the procession enter the church! Firecrackers burst, and everywhere there were arches of flowers.

Thus was Christmas Eve celebrated. The fiesta at the church was beautiful.

Ipan inin *novecientos* matlactli xihuitl yomomanaya
tianquiztli cuali. Nochtin tlanamacaquez yocuicaya xochicuali, achi cuacuali tzotzomatli huelez ican ye miactin
totlamachticatzitzintin yomehualhuiaya ompan Momochco.

Ye yiman on yomohtaya que melahuac nochtin chantlaca otlaneltocaya queni ca yazque cocone tlamachtilcalco. Aihmo ca oyaya nian tzatzapaltic nian tzoyo. Iqui in
ica yomomelauhta, momelauhtaque chantlaca. Aihmo
onyeya nian tetzacoz. Nian aihmo, tetzacuiloya ipampan
aihmo mohuicaya *pantalón*. Nochtlacatl yoquipiaya ipan-
talon ihuan cuali icoton. Nian tequixtililoz *multa*. Anca
nochtin piltzitzintin quen palomaxtoton tzicuintihue
ompan tlamachtilcalco.

XI. THE GOOD TEACHERS

And the village continues in its evolution. In the past, only the government authorities and the priest ruled. Today the school teachers voice their opinions.

By 1910, the market place had improved. There were merchants who brought fruit, and others brought woven materials. Perhaps all of this took place because many teachers were now living in the village.

By that time, it was clear that the people had decided to obey and were willing to send their children to school. Almost none of the children were ragged or dirty. They had taken the good path and gave an example to the people of the village. Men were no longer arrested or taken to jail for not wearing trousers. By this time, every man had his good trousers and a good shirt. They were no longer fined, because all the children ran off to school like little white doves.

But the parents of the boys and girls were called to-

Noihqui tlen cocone ichpocatoton ihuan telpocatoton occepa oquinmonochililique tatatzitzintin quename quimpiazque inimequez cocone. Ichpocatoton oquipiaya tlen tlecozque ica ipan *escalera* ipan ome *piso* tlamachtilcalco. Oquinmonochililique tatatin oncuan on ohcue quincahcohuizque, quinmediascohuizque ichpocame amo quitehtitizque in nacayo. Pipiltoton noihqui quipiazque icahhuan; ihuan motitizque quename nemizque ican ye telpocatoton ihuan ichpocatoton.

Tatatin amo zan niman otlaneltocaque. Oquinanquilique *inspector:* "Axcan titechmolhuilia tiquincahcohuizque ihuan tiquinmediascohuizque ichpocame, ican amo ticpia tomin huelez amo icihcan titlaneltocazque."

"Huel totlatlauhtia," omotelhuili in *inspector*, "ma ica *septiembre* ye yiman on nochtin cocone tlananquilizque ica icahhuan yeyencuicuez. Noihqui telpocatoton tlaneltocazque iman tica on. Tlacamo nantlanentocazque ticchihuazque que ye quezqui xihuitl: namechtzacuazque. ¡*Solo* iqui on namotitizque quename nantlaneltocazque!"

Ipan in xihuitl 1910 oniquimpix achi cuacuali notemachticahuan.

Ce momoztla otocuicatiaya iixpan acpatl; iixpan otocuicatiaya. Iman tica in tatatzitzintin ica nanatzitzintin oquipiaya tlen inixpan panoz tlen oquinmachtiaya piltzitintin. Oquintlatolmachtiaya caxtilancopa ihuan telpochtiazque nozo ichpochtiazque quimatizque quenemizque ihuan tlen quichihuazque.

Noihqui temachticahuan oquinmilhuiaya: "Nanquitla-

100

gether again and were given instructions about how they should bring up the young people. The girls had to walk up the staircase to the second floor of the school house, and the parents were told to buy them stockings to hide their legs. And the young boys had to wear shoes. All these orders were given so that the young people would learn how to live decently.

But the fathers and mothers did not obey immediately. They said to the principal, "You tell us to buy shoes for the boys and stockings for the girls, but since we have no money, we may not be able to obey very soon."

"We beg you!" the principal answered. "By this coming September the children must have new shoes to wear. And they must learn to be obedient. If you do not follow our orders, we will do what we did some years ago. We will put you in jail. That seems to be the only way you will learn to obey us!"

Around the year 1910, I had very good teachers.

Every day we sang to the flag. We sang there in front of it. It was then that the fathers and mothers began to realize that their children were learning. We were taught to speak Spanish and to know how to live a proper way of life. We were prepared to grow up as well-behaved young men and women.

"You must love your parents," the teachers said, "because they have toiled to send you to school." These were the words of the principal, and all his words reached our hearts.

zotlazque namotatzitzihuan ipampa yehuan motequipachozque ican namechtitlanizque tlamachticalco." Ihqui on
otechnonotzaya *inspector*; oncuan on toyolo oacia nochi
tlen itlatol otechnonotzaya.

Otlamia tlanonotzaliztli zan ica otexexeloaya. Tlen ce
año omocahuaya can otlatoc *inspector*. Ica ome *año*
otlecoya ica tlacpac can ocuachi tlamachtilcaltin oyeya.
Ihqui on omoxexeloaya coconentoton ica in tlamachtili
can onemachtiloya. Ihuan tla aca piltzitzintin nozo cihuantoton opanoaya occe xihuitl, iman on tlen axan quicuitia
pruebas (iman on oquicuitiaya *examen*). Ihuan tla cuali
oquiz ipan *examen*, iman on omomachtiaya temachtique.
Tlen amo oquizaya itoca-piltontli nozo cihuanton-yehuatl
on quitoznequia amo opanoc occe xihuitl ihuatl zan yompa
mocahuaz occepa.

Iman on ometztac inin tiatihuani Justo Sierras ihuan
mitoaya *Secretario de Educación*. Omotequipachoaya in-
pampa momachtiquez. Oncuan on mochicahuazque
tlazalozque. Ipan macuili tonali *mayo* otexexelhuiaya
premios, icahuiltoton ihuan yeyi nozo nahui amochtin achi
cualtzitzin. Nehuatl, niluz, hueyi onechtlatla colique ahuil-
toton ihuan amochtin. Cecenxihpa cuali oniquizaya ihuan
onechmacaya ce *diploma*.

Ca yipan xihuitl nochtin coconentoton oyaya tlamachtilcalco, cequi chichipahuaquez, cequi tzoyoquez.

Oquinotzque tatatin ihuan oquimilhuic *inspector:* "Inomequez cocone tzotzoyoquez, tla iqui on hualatazque
nochipa tiquintocazque inchan ihuan amo momachtizque.

102

When the talks had finished, all of us went home. When we were in the first grade, we stayed on the ground floor with the principal. In second grade, we went up to the second floor where there were other classrooms. The teachers and the children who were being educated were divided in that way. And if a boy or girl wished to go on to the next grade, they had to pass the exams. If we passed the exam, the teacher would call out our name. The boys and girls who were not named knew that they had not passed the grade and that they would have to do the same year over again.

A great man, Justo Sierra, was the Minister of Education in those times. He was completely devoted to see to the progress of the students in their studies. Every Fifth of May, prizes were awarded—toys and three or four beautiful books. I, Luz, received many things as gifts or prizes—playthings and books. I passed every grade and was given a diploma.

Around that year, all the children went to school, some washed but others still dirty.

The principal made all the parents appear before him, and he said, "If the children continue to come here unwashed, we will have to send them home and they will never get an education. Oh fathers and mothers, what do you say? Will you keep your children clean? Or must they be expelled from school? We, the teachers, want your children to grow up clean. Thus Milpa Alta will be great because the children will know how to read, write, and

¡Namehuan nantatatin! ¿Tlen nanquitoa? ¿Nanquimiceliz-que namopilhuan? ¿Nozo yazque de yipan tlamachtilcali? Tlen ticnequi tehuan titemachtiquez coconentoton hue-panhuizque chichipahuaque. Noihqui oncuan on hueyi yez Momochco Malacateticpac ica quimatizque momach-tizque, tlacuilozque ihuan tlapohuazque, noihqui tlacui-cuilozque itech amatl quicuitia *cartoncillo*. Tlemach cuacuali tlamachtili quizalozque. Oc tepitoton; ticnequi tiquinmictitizque que camicelizque ihuan tla namehuan nantatatin amo namotequipachoa, tehuan titemachtiquez coza totequipachoa impampa piltzitzintin quizalozque que ica nemizque. ¡Namehuan nantatatin nantlananquilizque ica coconentoton!"

Tatatin otelhuique: "¿Quenin timonequiltia, mahuiztic tlacatl, que hualazque chichipahuaque? Nian ipan toxolal amonca atl. Onca zan tepitzin; techtlacolitihue ome *bote* atl zan ce huiptlatica."

"Nehuatl nicmati," oquito *inspector*, "quename onca campa mocuiz atl. Zan cualcan nehualoz. Icuac aciz chi-cueyi tepoztlamachotiloni ica huatzincopa yotimaxitico ica atzintli. Caxilia piltzintli ica mixamiz, momatequiz ihuan moxopapacaz. Oncuan on motitiz quename hualaz chipahuac. Amo huel hueca: ca nochcalco, can petlantica hueyi atl. Tlacayo huiloa mocuiz atl ica nochcalco, ica tecomic. Occequi tlacatl huiloa ica San Gregorio Atla-pulco. Oncuan on amo tepoloz atl ica tlacualchihualoz, ica tlapacoz ihuan ica micelizque piltzitzintin tlen yahue tlamachtilcalco."

104

count. They will also know how to draw things on paper. They will learn good lessons. They are still small, but we want to teach them to be clean. And if you, the parents, are not interested in these things, we, the teachers, are. The boys and girls must learn to live properly. You, fathers and mothers, you must answer for them now!"

"Kind sir," the parents answered, "how can you demand that our children go to school clean? Water is scarce here in the village. There is very little water. All we can get is two containers of water every third day."

The principal answered, "I know where water can be obtained. It is just a question of getting up early. By eight o'clock in the morning, you will have returned with the water. The children will have sufficient water to wash their faces, hands, and feet. Thus they will learn to be clean. The place where the waters shine, Nochcalco, 'The Place of the House of the Prickly Pear Cactus,' is not far away. People go to fetch water from Nochcalco or Tecomitl. Others go to San Gregorio Atlapulco. There will be enough water to cook food and to wash the children who go to school.

"You have heard me, oh fathers and mothers! If at the beginning of next week, a single dirty child is sent to school, we will have to send him home. I beg you to listen to what I am telling you. We are going to turn out children who will become teachers or priests or lawyers. Others may have to find work far away from the village. When they grow to be young people, the girls who have gone to school

"Yonanquicaque ¡nantatatin ihuan nannanatin! Tla calaqui *semana* ihuan tlatzoyo hualaz conetl tictocazque ma yauh ichan. Huel miac namechtlatlauhtia nanquichi-huazque tlen namechilhuia. Oncuan on nian quizazque co-conentoton noihqui temachtiquez nozo totopixque nozo *licenciados* ihuan occequi cuacuali tequitizque cana oc-ceni. Nochin tlen momachtiquiuh icuac ye telpocatl nozo ichpocatl amo tetequipanoz campa ticiz nextamali, tlax-caloz huan itech tlapactel yetaz."

"¿Amo namechtlacoltia quenamehuan nanquipano? Tla nanquimatizquia amatl achi occe cuali tequitl nan-quipiazquia. Huel miac namechilhuia itech xitlachacan inimequez cocone. Namehuan nanhuehuetizque ihuan namopilhuan amo namechequictazque ipampa amo cuali omomachtique."

"Axcan nancuica namopilhuan tlacualizpa ihuan nan-quincahuaquihue ipan ome tlamachotiloni teotlac quiza-lozque tlacuicuilozque, tlatetequizque, mocuicatizque. Nochin quizalozque teotlac. Occequi cuacuali tlamachtili quizalozque quename panotihue ipan xiuhtin. Ihqui on conetl ye cuica itic itzonteco nochi tlen omomachti ihuan tla moztla, huiptla nanmimiquizque tatatin, yehuan ye quimatizque que quitematomazque quezqui melio. Ica on namechtlatlauhtia huel miac nanquichihuazque tlen namechilhuia."

will not have to become servants—grinding corn, kneading dough for tortillas, slaves of the washboard.

"Are you not ashamed at the way in which you are spending your lives? Are you not sorry for yourselves? If you knew how to read and write, you would have a much better position in life. I insist that you look out for your children. You will grow old, and your children will turn their backs on you because you did not give them an education.

"Now you must take away your children at noon and bring them back to school at two o'clock in the afternoon so they may learn how to draw, cut out clothing, and sing. They will learn all these things in the afternoon. They will also learn other useful things as the years go by. Then the children will remember everything they have learned, and if their parents die tomorrow or the day after, the children will know how to make a living. I beg you to follow my advice."

In cahchichiquez oyeya ompan Momochco Malacatepec. Cetzin ipan *barrio* San Mateo, occetzin San Juan Iztayopan omotlacatili ihuan omocihuauhtitzino noihqui ompan San Mateo itlac ce cuali ichpocatl. Nochi imacopatian. Inimequez tlatihuanime omotecahchichihuiliaya ihuan amo patio omotlaniliaya. Omotelhuiliaya chicome tonali tiquimaniliquiuh cacahtin. Cualtzitzin cahtin, axcan mocuitia *choclo*. Oyeya noihqui achi cualtzitzin cualtoton cahtin: ocuicaya botontin *desde* tlaxitla *hasta* tlacpac.

XII. THE CENTENNIAL

As the sixteenth of September draws near, the Republic prepares to celebrate the one hundredth anniversary of Hidalgo's struggle for independence. In the Capital, Don Porfirio will soon be congratulated on his eightieth birthday. Justo Sierra founds the National University. Mexico is now a modern nation, "the treasure house of the world," and Díaz is "the greatest man on the Continent." Diplomats from Europe, Asia, and Africa, from the United States and the other American nations, all are ready to begin the long voyage to Mexico to applaud the great man and admire the wealth and progress of the country.

But the Centennial is the last flicker of a dying flame. The regime faces international complications, a financial crisis, internal political intrigue, the strong opposition of labor and peasantry, and the decrepitude of the Father of Modern Mexico.

Meanwhile Milpa Alta prepares for the great day.

There were shoemakers in Milpa Alta. One was from the quarter of San Mateo. The other was a native of San Juan Iztayopan, but he was married to a fine girl from San Mateo. They did all their work well. These men made shoes, and they were not expensive. They told the customers to come back to get their shoes in about a week. Beautiful shoes they were. Today we call them *choclos*. There were also other fine shoes with buttons running from top to bottom. Still others were adorned with finery and

Noihqui oyeya occequintin oquintlatlachaltiaya. Ica macehualcopa mitoaya zayoltoton de tepoztli ihuan noihqui
botontin oquicaya *desde* tlaxitla *hasta* tlapac. Occequintin
noihqui b otastin ican *abujetas* achi cualtzitzin omohtaya.
Inimequez cahchiquez oquipixque hueyi tequitl ipampan oquipiaya tlen tlaneltocazque piltzitzintin ihuan tatatin moteixmachtizque quename tlaneltocani. Opehque
cahchiquez quinchichihua *desde* ipan metztli *mayo*, ihuan
icuac oacic tonali caxtoli ihuan ce *septiembre* nochtin
cocone yoquipiaya icahtoton. Oncuan on amoca yaz *sin*
cahtli tlamachtilcalco. Nochtlacatl onemauhtiloya ipampan tlacamo tlaneltocoz quintzatzacuazque tatatin ce
metztli nozo miaque tomin quixtlahuatihue ompan *prefectura*. Ica on nochtlacatl omotequipacho quicahtiz inpilhuan.

"Inin tonali," oquihto *inspector* tatatin ihuan piltzitzintin, "nanquilnamiquizque icuac caxiltiz ce *siglo* icuac
aihmo otechmoxopechtique in cuitlaxcoliztaque inimequez quimilhuia *españoles*. Tlanonotzalo tocoltzitzihuan
quename cuitlaxcoliztaque oquitotomaya tepoztli totonqui
ihuan oquintlatlatiaya macehualtin nozo mexicatlaca.
Ipampa in nicnequi nochtin pipiltzitzintin ihuan namehua
nanquitlalizque ipan namoyolo tlen tocoltzitzihuan omo-
papanoltique. Hueyi quitoznequi caxtoli ihuan ce tonali
septiembre. ¡Caxiltiz ce *cientos* icuac omotlan *guerra!*"

"Icayon tihnequi cocone quizalozque ce cuicatl achi
cualtzin can yolehuaz namoyolo inon tonali. Ipampa on

110

were called *zayoltoton de tepoztli* (little metal flies). They also had buttons running from top to bottom. There were also laced boots, something fine to see.

These shoemakers had plenty of work to do since they had to labor for both the children and their parents, who by now had learned to obey. The shoemakers began their task in the month of May and by the sixteenth of September, the children had their shoes ready. On that great day, not a child was to go to school barefooted. The people had been given a scare. If the fathers and mothers did not obey, they were to be jailed for a month or they would have to pay a large fine to the village government. That is why all hurried to have shoes made for their children.

"Today," the principal said to the parents and children, "you will remember that a century has passed since we were slaves of the whites called Spaniards. Our grand-parents told us that the whites heated irons and burned the Indians or Mexicans with them. So, I want you and your children to remember the sufferings of our ancestors in your hearts. The sixteenth of September will be a day we shall never forget! A century has passed since the end of the wars!

"Therefore we want the children to learn a wonderful song—a song to thrill hearts on that day. We want the girls to be dressed in white with a ribbon in the colors of the flag over their shoulders. The boys will wear white trousers and white shirts and a ribbon with the flag's colors on one arm.

111

tihnequi hualazque cihuantoton ica iztac intzotzoma ihuan quicuitlalpizque ca se *listón* can hualaz que inon pantli. Pipiltoton cualicazque in pantalonhuan iztaque, incotontoton noihqui iztaque. Itech ima hualilpitaz noihqui *listón* quename pantli. Ica yehuatl on cuicatl mocuicatizque. ¡Ican caxilia ce *cientos* xihuitl Mexico!"

"Noihqui totatzin *presidente* Porfirio Díaz ihuan huey tlatihuani Justo Sierras quinmotetlacolilizque medayatin can icuilcatica 'In Centenario'."

"Ome nozo yeyi metztli quipia nochtin tlen momachtizque in cuicatl. Huel miac namechtlatlauhtia macamo ca tlacotona nian ce tonali. Oncuan on cuali quizaz cuicatl. Amoca moixpoloz, amoca motlapololtiz ihuan cuali quitoz cuicatl."

Ye yiman oyecoc tonali icuac coconentoton opaquiya omononotzaya nochtin ipan tlamachtilcali:

"¿Yomitzin cencahuilique mocahhuan?"

"Nehuatl yonpacate nocahhuan."

Tzatzatzi nochtin cocone, noihqui tehuan "¡Nochi yompaca totzotzomahhuan, cahtin ica mediastin!"

Nochi totatzitzihuan ica yomotlalitzinoque. "Aihmo tlatechpoloa; ye yiman ye huitz caxtoli ihuan ce tonali *septiembre*."

Quilnamique cocone tlen oquimilhuique tatatin "¡namechtzacuazque!"

"Za chicueyi tonali techpoloa taquizque yencuic totzotzoma. ¡Nochi, nochi yencuic! Amotla itzoltic nozo tzatza-

112

Then they will sing the hymn. Mexico is going to celebrate its hundredth year on that day!

"Our Father, the President Porfirio Díaz and the great señor Justo Sierra will give us gifts: medals inscribed with the words 'The Centennial.'

"All the children will have to rehearse the song for two or three months, and I do not want anyone to be absent a single day. Thus no one will make a single mistake, and the song will be perfect."

And the day came when the children started talking among themselves in school.

"Have they finished your shoes?"

"Yes, my shoes are ready."

All the boys yelled with excitement, and we girls also yelled. "Our dresses are ready! And so are our shoes and stockings!"

All our fathers and mothers made preparations. "Nothing is lacking now. The sixteenth of September is coming!"

The children remembered the warning given to their parents: "If you do not obey, we will put you in jail."

"A week from now we will be wearing our new clothes! And all of them will be new. Nothing will be torn or ragged! And there is still more to come—the gifts we are to get at school!"

The clothes sent by Justo Sierra arrived in a cart. The names of the poor children, together with a list of what

paltic. Axan polihui tlen techtlacolizque ompan tlamachtilcalco."

Oacico tzotzomatli noihqui ce tepoztlahuilanalali
oquititlan *don* Justo Sierra. Ihuan tlen ihnococone oyi-
cuilactaya itech ce amatl tlen itoca cocone, tlen quintlaco-
lizque. Can oacic tonali oquinmacaque in coton, in
xolochcue.

Mexico mahuiztictlacatl *presidente* ihuan Justo Sierra
huelez omihtalhuiaya que amo tlaneltocoz ihuan oquiti-
tlanilique tzotzomatli ihuan cahtin. Miaque cocone aihmo
oquinequia tzotzomatli tlen omotitlanique *secretarios*
ipampa nochtin tatatin otlaneltocaque.

Nehuatl niluz noihqui oniyeya ipan macuili xihuitl
onomachtitaya, tlen axan quicuitia *quinto año.* Onechtla-
colique nocahhuan, noxolochcue ihuan nocoton ipampa
notatzitzihuan noihqui ihnotlacame.

Oacic tonali in caxtoli ihuan ce in metztli *septiembre.*
Oacito coconentoton tlamachtilcalco. Nochtin pipiltzitzintin ica ichpocatoton oacito tlamachtilcalco cacpipitzca;
nochtin. Ihuan nican yoyecoc tzotzomatli tlen quinmama-
cazque icnotlacacocone. Ipan caxtoli ihuan ce tonali
septiembre otlaehualolo ica pantli ihuan ixpan pantli
omocuicatique cocone. Ihuan iman on oquinxexelhuique
diplomas tlen cualoquizque ipan xihuitl.

Ican totaca yocuilactaya tlen in omanili *inspector* amatl
ihuan monenehuiliaya tlen itoca cihuanton nozo piltontli.
Otlecoya ipan ce cuauhtlapechtli. Ihuan ompoyon omotle-

114

they were to receive, were written on paper. When the day came, the gifts were distributed—shirts and dresses.

In the city of Mexico the good president and the minister had thought, perhaps, that no one would obey them. That is why they sent clothes and shoes. Many children no longer needed the clothing that the minister sent, since almost all the parents had already obeyed.

I, Luz, was in the fifth grade at that time. I was given shoes, a dress, and a blouse, because my parents were very poor.

Then came the sixteenth of September. The children arrived at school. All the boys and girls went to school, their shoes so new that they squeaked. And then arrived the clothing that was to be given to the children of the poor. On the sixteenth, the entire village gathered around the flag while the children sang. And then diplomas were given to those who had passed the school year.

Then the principal took the piece of paper on which the children's names were written, and he began to call the names of the boys and girls. They had to walk up on a wooden platform. They went up and then new names were called out. The children went up the steps of the platform. They went up four by four and came down on the other side. More and more boys and girls! They walked up on the platform where they were given clothing according to the list.

Many—those who were barefooted—were given shoes,

115

cahuic ihuan oquinmotenehuiliaya. Otlecoyac cocone, nahui coconentoton otlecozque ihuan ica occecni temoz-qui. Occepa oquinmotenehuiliaya tlen itoca pipiltoton ihuan cihuantoton. Otlecoya ompa cuauhtlapechco can oquinmacaya in tzotzoma tlen ohuali icuilauhtaya itech amatl.

Miactin oquinmamacaque cactin, tlen inomequez zan chichipahuaque icxiton oyaya. Yehuan on ompa oquima-quique cactin. Ihuan tla oquinmacazque tzotzomatli noihqui oquintlaquiaya.

Ican omotac ica miactin cocone opopolahuia itic tla-machtilcalco Momochco Malacatepec ohualtemoque momachtiquez *desde* Tupilejo, San Pablo Oztotepec, San Pedro Atocpan, Santa Ana Tlacotenco, San Lorenzo Tlacoyuca, San Francisco Tecozpa, San Jerónimo Mia-catlan ihuan San Juan Tepenahuac. Nochtinin cocone ocacahuania ipan Milpa Alta.

Ica on huehueyi tlaca aihmo oquintlalique cocone zan oquinmamacaya tlen in huaxca: in xolochcue, in coton huan incahhuan. Ipampa miaque cocone oyeya omone-milique *inspector* ican *autoridades* aihmo quinmamacaz-que ica tihualotaz ipampa tlatozque nochi in tlatihuanime ihuan hueyi tlatoli.

Ihuan omolhuili:

¡Pantli Mexico, pantli!

Quilton, iztac ihuan chichiltic pantli.

¡In Mexico azcatl!

116

and the shoes were put on them. And if they needed clothing, they were dressed right there on the spot.

When they saw that a great number of boys and girls had gathered at the school of Milpa Alta, other school children started coming in from Topilejo, San Pablo Oztotepec, San Pedro Atocpan, Santa Ana Tlacotenco, San Lorenzo Tlacoyuca, San Francisco Tecozpa, San Jeronimo Miacatlan, and San Juan Tepenahuac. All these children made a great deal of noise in Milpa Alta.

By this time, the authorities had stopped dressing the children on the spot. They were given only what was theirs —skirts, shirts, and shoes. Because the children were many, the principal and the authorities decided not to keep them standing because all the dignitaries were to deliver speeches. And they were to be long speeches!

Then came the recitation:

Mexican banner, Mexican flag—
Green, white and red!
The flag of Mexico!
This day, this month, this year,
You are one hundred years old
They, the peasants, remember the blood
Shed a century ago,
When our father Hidalgo freed us from the white skins,
From the Spaniards.
We give our hearts to you

117

Inin tonali, inin metztli ihuan inin xihuitl
ticaxiltia macuilpohuali xihuitl.

Yehuan, mamacehualtin quilnamiqui tlen yeztli onenen
axacan ce *siglo*, icuac totatzin Hidalgo otechmoquiquix-
tili in xopaltech *españoles* nozo cuitlaxcoliztac.

Tictemaca ca nochi toyolo quiyezque nochipa tlamach
ihuan timitzehualozque quename yetic ihuan quename
ce tlazotli techipahuac nantli oncuan Mexico quitlaniz
in *victoria* ihuan aihmo ca in xopaltiz tiyezque.

Ihuan omocuicac:

> *Surgir de humildes cunas*
> *y en santos ideales*
> *para vivir hasta los hechos:*
> *es obra de abnegados,*
> *es obra de colosos,*
> *que nacen para gloria*
> *y orgullo de los pueblos.*

Opehque zan niman quixexeloa *premios de* tlen oc
hualoquizque ipan occe xihuitl otipanoque. Ihuan onech-
macaque ce *diploma* cano icuilactaya "NEHUATL, NIPOR-
FIRIO DIAZ, ALTEPETL MEXICO, IPAN ITOCA TOTLALNAN-
TZIN, NICTEXEXELHUIA INIMEQUEZ MEDAYATIN IPAMPA
MOMACHTIA COCONE, ONCUAN ON AIH QUILCAHUAZQUE
TLEN QUINMACA IN TZONTECO CUALI MOMACHTIA."

Ihuan otlan tlaxexeloliztli *premios* zan aca iman on
omoxexeloque medayatin cano icuilactaya quename "cax-

118

and we will be loyal to one another forever.
We stand around you
As if you were our loving mother.
Mexico will win all the victories!
No one will come to step on us again!

Then prizes were awarded to those who had passed to the next grade. I was given a diploma and the words were there: "I, PORFIRIO DIAZ, RULER OF MEXICO, AWARD THESE MEDALS IN THE NAME OF OUR COUNTRY TO THE CHILDREN WHO HAVE LEARNED THEIR LESSONS WELL. LET THEM NEVER FORGET WHAT THEY HAVE RECEIVED, WHAT THEY HAVE BEEN TAUGHT."

The distribution of prizes ended and the medals were awarded. Each one of them bore an inscription: "MEXICO IS ONE HUNDRED YEARS OLD. THIS IS THE CENTENNIAL." The sun shone bright. It was very warm. Then we began our song:

> Oh holy banner,
> Your heroic colors remind us of
> The red, generous blood,
> Shed by our heroes,
> The splendid green of our forests,
> The white snows of our mountains!
>
> Should the woes of the past
> Return to trouble you,

iltia ce *siglo* Mexico: in *Centenario.*" Tlamia in tonali in
Centenario ica tlacualiztli. Achi cualtzin tonali oyeya;
otonataya coza. Oncuan on ompeuh cuicatl:

*¡Oh santa bandera
de heroicos carmines!
Suben a la gloria
de tus tafetanes
la sangre abnegada
de los paladines,
el verde pomposo
de nuestros jardines
¡las nieves sin mancha
de nuestros volcanes!*

*Si tornan las luchas
de ayer a tus plantas
sobre nuestros ojos
de sombras cubiertos,
recuerda, bandera,
la sangre abnegada
de los paladines,
el verde pomposo
de nuestros jardines,
¡las nieves sin mancha
de nuestros volcanes!*

Should our eyes
Be covered with shadows again!
Remember, oh banner
The red, generous blood shed by our heroes,
The splendid green of our forests,
The white snows of our mountains!

PART TWO: THE REVOLUTION

Amo otlacualoc oncan techtlanahualiz quename ye huitz atlatlacamamaniliztli. Amo otimatiaya hueyi quiahuitl ihuan de tlacatecolotl. [...]

[...] tlatihuani Zapata Morelos. Ihuan omixmatia ican cuali itzotzoma ocualicaya. Oquipiaya ce calacecahuili patlactic, *polainas* ihuan [...] Itlacahuan oquipiaya intzotzoma nochi iztac: icoton iztac, icalzon iztac ihuan tecahtin. Inimequez tlaca nochtin otlatoaya macehualcopa [...] Noihqui tlatihuani Zapata omotlatoltiaya in macehualatoli. Ica on icuac omocalaquia in Milpa Alta nochtlacatl oquicaquia tlen omitalhuiaya. Inimequez *zapatistas* oquipiaya in calacecahuil; itech oquintlaliliaya tlen isanto oquitlazotlaya oncuanon quipalehuiz. Nochtin iqui on ohualaya in calacecahuil ica *santo*.

124

XIII. THE MEN OF THE SOUTH

Deafened by the ringing of bells, military bands, parades, and weary of noise, Mexico City sleeps profoundly on the night of the sixteenth of September, 1910. The people of Milpa Alta also sleep, though their ears still ring with the din of the band, the songs of the school children, and the pompous speeches of the prefect and the professors. In San Miguel Anenecuilco, Morelos, far away from Milpa Alta, there also sleeps a Nahuatl-speaking Indian: Emiliano Zapata.

But let us permit Doña Luz, who received her Porfirian medal so proudly in 1910, to speak for herself:

The heavens did not thunder to warn us that the tempest was coming. We knew nothing about the storms nor about the owlish wickedness of men.

One day gunfire was heard between the hills of Teuhtli and Cuauhtzin. We were told that it was the Federals fighting against the men of Morelos. There was a lot of shooting. It was the first time we had heard such a thing, and all of Milpa Alta trembled.

The men of Morelos kept passing through the village, and it was said they were on their way to Xochimilco. I do not know why they were against Porfirio Díaz.

These men from Cuernavaca and Tepoztlan spoke our language. They were only peasants, and we did not know why the Federals were afraid of them.

125

Tlatihuani Zapata oquimecanaya itlacahuan. Ocalaquia quinonotzaya nochtlacatl Momochco. "¡Notlac ximomanaca! Nehuatl onacoc; oncuan on ica tepoztli ihuan nochantlaca niquinhuicatz. Ipampa in Totatzin Díaz aihmo ticnequi yehuatl techixotiz. Ticnequi occe altepetl achi cuali. Ihuan totlac ximomanaca ipampa amo nechpactia tlen tetlaxtlahuia tlatquihua. Amo conehui ica tlacualo ica netzotzomatiloz. Noihqui nicnequi nochtlacatl quipiaz itlal: oncuan on quitocaz ihuan quipixcaz tlaoli, yetzintli ihuan occequi xinachtli. ¿Tlen nanquitoa? ¿Namehuan totlac namomanazque?"

Ayemo ca otlananquili. Ihuan opanoc tonaltin. Oquitlalique in *cuartel* Zapata ihuan Everardo González. Inin tlatihuani omocauh oncuan quixotiz in Momochco Malacateticpac.

Iqui on oquinamiquiliaya in *general* Zapata. Oquinchihualtiaya nochi altepeme quinamiquitihui in *general*. Miac tlaca ihuan cihuame ica xochitl ihuan musicatin tlatzotzonazque ihuan oquicuecuepotzaya in *cuete* icuac calaquiz ihuan quitzotzonazque *diana*.

Opapanoque iquin cequintin metzli ihuan Totatzin Porfirio Díaz ica *secretario* Justo Sierras amo omotequipachoaya ipampa huitz *revolución*. Zan oncuan oquintlazotlaya nochi mexicatlaca ica mexicacocone. Campa oyeya nahui piltzitzintin oquintlacoliaya tzotzomatli. Tla cihuanton oquimacaya icoton ihuan ixolochcue; ihuan tla piltontli oquimacaya icamisa ihuan ce *pantalón*.

Huelez omitalhuilaya tlatihuanitzitzintin Díaz ihuan

126

This was the first thing we heard of the Revolution. One day a great man by the name of Zapata arrived from Morelos. He wore good clothes—a fine broad hat and spats. He was the first great man to speak to us in Nahuatl. All his men were dressed in white—white shirts, white pants, and they all wore sandals. All these men spoke Nahuatl more or less as we spoke it. Señor Zapata also spoke Nahuatl. When all these men entered Milpa Alta, we understood what they said. Each of the Zapatistas carried pinned to his hat a picture of his favorite saint, so that the saint would protect him. Each bore a saint in his hat.

Zapata stood at the head of his men and addressed the people of Milpa Alta in the following way: "Come join me! I have risen in arms, and I have brought my countrymen with me. We don't want Our Father Díaz to watch over us any more. We want a better president to care for us. Join the Revolution with us since we are tired of the few cents the rich pay us. There isn't enough to eat or to buy clothes. I want every man to have his own plot of land. He will sow it and reap corn, beans, and other grains. What do you people say? Will you join us?"

Nobody answered. The days passed. The barracks of Zapata and Everardo González were set up in the village. González was told to stay in Milpa Alta to watch over the village.

General Zapata was received in the following way. Everyone in the village went out to receive him. Crowds of

Sierras: "Iquin ica motitizque tatatin ihuan nanantin que ica quimpiazque coconentoton ihuan ica quititlanizque tlamachtilcalco."

Iqui melahuac tlen omonemililique mahuiztic tlaca; iqui on otlananquilique nochtlacatl.

Ca ipan inin xihuitl yopehuaya motenehuaz quename yomacohtaya ica Chihuahua Madero, Carranza huan Obregón. Ica tlaxitla ma tiquitocan ica Cuauhnahuac noihqui yomotenehuaya in *revolución*; ancan ayemo machiaya ahquen oquipehualtiaya.

men and women came with flowers in their hands. A band played and fireworks burst; and when he had entered, the band played the *diana*.

Several months went by, and Our Father Porfirio Díaz and the Secretary Justo Sierra were not worried about the Revolution. Their great passion was the Mexican people. Wherever there were four children, they were given clothing. Girls were given a blouse and a skirt, and boys were given a shirt and trousers.

Perhaps Señores Díaz and Sierra believed this: "Fathers and mothers will thus learn how to give an education to their children. They will send them to school."

The hopes of these great men were fulfilled, and everybody in the village obeyed them.

Inin tlatihuani Everardo ma tiquitocan yehuatl oquinte-
quihtiaya nochi in *pueblo* quitetla colizque tlaxcali, atl
ihuan tlacuali *para* yolcame. Huan quicahuatihue ompan
cuartel. Nochtlacatl otlaneltocaya. Huatzinco, teotlac,
oyaya tlacuali *para zapatistas* ihuan yolcame. Ipan in
tonaltin oquimiquilique *don* Abraham Monterola hue'ca.
Ayoquic omachix, tla oquimomictilique. Noihqui tlatihuani itoca Juan Bastida; noihqui oquimiquilique. Ayoquic omachix canon necahualo.

Inin tlatihuani Everardo oquinmonochiliaya inon tlaca
tlatquihuatoton ihuan oquilhuiaya: "Titechmacaz tomin;
¡tlacamo timitzmictizque!"

Cetzin tlatihuani notiotzin onechmononochili quename
oquinmolhuilic *don* Everardo: "Titechmacaz in tomin;

XIV. ZAPATA'S LIEUTENANT

In 1911 the President and his Minister of Education flee to Europe. Unaware of the causes that had led Mexico to enter a new and violent era, Justo Sierra dies in Madrid in 1912 and Porfirio Díaz in Paris in 1915. But the words of Justo Sierra still echo in Mexico: "The people of Mexico hunger and thirst for justice."

Several presidents rule in the Capital: Francisco León de la Barra, Francisco I. Madero, Pedro Lascuráin and Victoriano Huerta. The Nahuatl speaking world of the south of the Federal District, in its isolation, cannot follow the tragic events which occur in Mexico City between 1911 and 1915. Milpa Alta considers the Revolution to be a struggle between the Zapatistas of Morelos and the military regimes which rule over the Capital.

Don Everardo was the general Zapata left in charge of the village. Everyone was to give him—free—tortillas, water, and fodder for the horses and mules. Each district of Milpa Alta had to carry these things to the soldiers' quarters, and all obeyed. Morning and afternoon people took food to the men of Zapata and to their animals. It was about that time that the Zapatistas kidnapped Don Abrán Monterola, and it was never discovered whether they murdered him or not. Another man, Juan Bastida, also disappeared. We never found out what became of them.

This man Everardo summoned the rich to him saying, "You are going to give us money. If you don't, we will kill you."

¡tlacamo timitztlatzontequilizque!" Notio omotlananquili: "Amo nicpiatomin ipampa nocihuauh ica nopilhuan yotlecoque ica Tepoztlan. Miaque tlaca ihuan cihuame oyahque ica Tepoztlan ihuan Amantlan. Nochi tomin ocuicaque ica tlacuazque ican amo ca quixmati Tepoztlan." Iman on oquitoc tlatihuani Everardo: "Amo nimitzmictiz ican yotitito tlen melahuac." Ihuan nonantzin nehuatl omicac omotlatlatlauhtilito itlac *don* Everardo noihqui, macamo quimomictilican ican quimpia miaque tepilhuan. In *don* Everardo aihmo quimictic *don* Regino notiotzin. Zan oquimotlalilique quimixotiliz ce *general* mihque. Amo omachix ahquen oquimihtic ihuan otlanahuatique itlac *don* Everardo quename ompa huetztoc ce *general*. Oquipiaya itepoztlamachotiloni *de oro*. Huan oquimolhuilique notio: "Tla aca quiquixtiliz, ye yiman on timiquiz."

Ce tonaltica otemoque *zapatistas* ihuan oquitliquechique *prefectura* ihuan *juzgado civil* ihuan cequi caltin. Inin ce cali tlatihuani tlatquihua itocatzin Luis Sevilla. Oquimocalatitique. Tetlacolti: cuecuepotzaya tlaoli, ahuax, yetzintli ihuan yolcame noihqui olihuahque ipan on cali. Occe tonaltica otemoque *zapatistas* ipan altepetl ihuan oquinquitzquiaya tlaca ican quintlamacatihue cahuatin ihuan quimatlitizque. Ye on oquichihuaya *zapatistas*.

Icuac ocalaque cuali cuali ipan xihuitl in *zapatistas* otlamimictique. Inimequez oquinmictiaya tlatquihuaz ican oquitlania tomin ihuan amo quinmacaya. Ye yiman on ocuicaya tlatihuani ihuan oquimictiaya ica cuauhtlatli.

I had an uncle who told me about the way Don Everardo talked to him. "You'll give us money, or we'll chop off your head."

"I have no money," my uncle answered, "and my wife and children have gone up to Tepoztlan. Many men and women have fled towards Tepoztlan and Amantla. They took all the money with them in order to survive. They don't know anyone in Tepoztlan."

"I am not going to kill you," Don Everardo said, "because you have spoken the truth."

My mother also went to beg Don Everardo not to kill him because he was a man with many children. So Don Everardo did not kill my uncle Regino. At that time, a general had been killed. His men went to tell Don Everardo that the general was lying on the ground. Don Everardo ordered my uncle to keep vigil over the corpse of the general, who still wore his gold watch. "If anyone steals that watch," my uncle was told, "you will die!" And so it was that my uncle had to stay up all night with the body of the general.

One day the Zapatistas came down and burned the town hall, the courthouse, and several homes. One of these houses belonged to a rich man by the name of Luis Sevilla.

His house was burned to the ground. It was enough to break your heart to hear the bursting of the grains of corn and the beans. All his domestic animals died in the burning of that house. The next day, the Zapatistas came down again to the village and forced our men to take fodder and

133

Noihqui oquinmichtequia ichpocame. Otlanonotzaloya que oquinhuicaya ica cuauhtla inca omahuiltiaya. Aihmo ce tonali ohualaya intlac itatzitzihuan. Oixpolihuia ica cuauhtla. Cox oquicuaya tecuani nozo oquintocaya, amo machia.

water to their horses. All of these things were caused by the Zapatistas.

When the men of Zapata entered the town, they came to kill. They killed the rich because they asked for large amounts of money which the rich were not willing to give up. Then they would take the rich men to the woods and murder them there. They also carried off girls. People said that they took them to the woods and raped them there. These maidens were abandoned forever in the woods, never to return to their homes. No one knew whether they were devoured by wild animals or whether the Zapatistas murdered and buried them there.

Ye yipan tica in opehque calaquizque ompan Momochco Malacatepec inimequez quicuitiaya otomites ihuan zapotecaz. Inimequez cihuame oquiyolaliaya inamihuan yehuan. Tlaca oyaya intlac *zapatistas*. Noihqui otlatoaya otomite ihuan occequintin cihuame otlatoaya mitoa zapoteca. Ihuan tlaxcali oquicuitiaya "chúzcuta." Occequi tlatoli otlatoaya; nehuatl amo nicaqui cuali tlen quitoznequi inon tlatoltin. Iman *zapatistas* oyatinemia ica ompa miaque tlatoltin. Oticaquia mononotza; molhuia ihuan zan yehuatzin toteco *Dios* momachtiaya tlen quitoa.

Inimequez cihuame ica tlaca noncuaca zapatistacayotl ihuan noncua oyeya tequitl. Tlaca ica cihuame omomamaya ica xoctin ica piltzitzintin ihuan otlecoya cuauhtla. Oconquixtiaya oconelhuatl ma tiquitocan yehuan in

XV. THE TEMPEST

All Mexico is shaken by the storm which has destroyed the old regime. Thousands of indigenous groups who have never seen beyond the mountains that enclose them move to and fro in the confusion of the moment. New languages are heard in Milpa Alta.

It was around that time that people speaking Otomí and Zapotec began to enter Milpa Alta. Women accompanied their husbands. These men came with the Zapatistas. They spoke what is called Otomí, and some of the women spoke Zapotec. They called the *tlaxcalli* (tortilla) "chúzcuta." New languages were heard, but I did not understand any of them. Different tongues were spoken in the village when the men of Zapata were there. We could hear them talking. They talked among themselves, but only God Our Lord knows what they were talking about.

These Otomí women and their husbands had come with the forces of Zapata. They lived a life of their own in the village. Men and women would load their pots and children on their backs and take off for the woods to pick ocote pine roots. It can be said that they were the ones who taught us the proper use of the root of the ocote pine. The men carried their shotguns since they came with the troops of Zapata. They shot rabbits and their women went to sell them in the city of Mexico. The Otomí were very good at that sort of thing.

137

oquiteititito tlen itech monequiz oconelhuatl. Tlaca oyaya ica tepoztlacueponili ican oyeya intlac Zapata. [. . .]

Noihqui oyaya tlanamacazque oquihuicaya xochicuali, chilchotl ihuan xonacatl. Ica yiman tica on ayemo ca Milpa Alta omocalactiaya coza tlanamacoz ipan tianquiztli. Ma opinaoaloya tochantlaca.

Inimequez cihuame omaquiaya coton ihuan tzomicueitl quechquemitl ihuan oyaya tlatianquizozque tianquizco. Oquichichihuaya in payo que ce *rueda* ihuan oquicuatihpanoya, quename motlacecahuiaya ica payo.

Ye yiman in ocalahque *zapatistas* ompan Amilco. Oquintlacalque achi miac *bombas* ica *ametralladoras* can oquitlacalque ome tlamachtilcaltin. Ye yiman tica on miactin *federales* omotlalpachoque icuac oxitinque caltin. Inimequez tlamachtilcaltin: cente itocan Concepción Arenal ihuan de pipiltoton aihmo niquilnamiqui tlen itoca. Ipan inin tlamachtilcali otlalpachihque miaque *federales* ican *soldaderas*.

Noihqui nocal oquitlatique *zapatistas* ipampa onichantia in cecatitla *cuartel federales*. Ye yiman tica in otlamimihtique in *zapatistas*; quen otlatechayauhtaya in *federales*.

Opanoya ce aca oquinequia panoz in ihpac mimiquez. Noihqui tlacayo tlachantlaca omimihqui ican zan tlalhuiz omocuecuepotzaya. Ce ichpocatl ipan tlapantli ompa ihtic ical ocaxili tepoztlacueponili ihuan zan niman omic. Ihqui on occequi tlaca omimiquia.

Aihmo omocauh in *federal* ica xolalpampa. Ye yiman

138

They also carried fruit, green chile, and onions to sell in the city of Mexico. In those times, the people of Milpa Alta were not good as traders. The people of the village were shy.

These Otomí women used to put on their blouses, their wrap-around skirts, and their *quechquemitls* and used to go off to buy and sell in the market place. They twisted their rebozos into rings and placed them around their heads. These rings gave them shade.

It was at this time that the men of Zapata came in, through the village of Amilco. Bombs and machine guns burst, and our two schools were destroyed. When these two buildings collapsed, many federal soldiers were buried in their ruins. One of the schools was called Concepción Arenal, and I do not remember the name of the boys' school. The federal soldiers were crushed to death, together with their camp followers, in my school—in the same classroom where I had learned so many things.

My home was also burned down by Zapata because I lived next to the barracks of the federals. The Zapatistas were killing federals until their corpses were like pebbles scattered on the ground.

If we wished to walk in the street, we had to walk over corpses. Many of the villagers were killed since the firing was done with little aim. A girl, standing on the roof of her house, was hit by a bullet and died a little while later. Many other people were slain in the same way.

tica on *zapatistas* otlecoque ipan tepetl Teuhtzin. Oquinchololtique *federales* ica San Gregorio, Xochimilco mate
oquimaxitique ompan Churubusco.

Carrancistas amo mitoaya calaquizque.

Nehuatl onicpiaya mactlactli ihuan nahui xihuitl ihuan
tetlac onomauhtic ican coza otlacuecuepotzaya. Ipan
tepetl Teuhtli, Tijeras ihuan Ocpayocan omomanaya
zapatistas.

Iman on ica ipan yeyi tetepe oquehualoque in *federales*.
Oquinchololtique ica cuauhtla. Cequi oyaque ica San
Pablo Oztotepec. Oacito ipan tepetl itocan Cuauhtzin.
Ompoyon omomanque achi miac *zapatistas*: omotlatitaya
ipan tetepe. Iman on yoquitaque ipanotica *federales*.
Zapatistas opeuhque quincuecuepotza. Ompoyon otlan-
que achi miaque. Ocholoque yeyi nozo nahui *federales*.
Oacique Milpa Alta ihuan ompa yoyeya ocuachi *federales*;
oquintitla *general* Díaz.

Occepa oquincaque ipan altepetl ye popolohui *zapatistas*. Ica occepa yomomanque ihuan zancual cantica quin-
tlatlatoltiaya in *federales*. Quincueponiaya noihqui; otlananquiliaya ica tepoztlacueponili. Ihquion oyeque cana
yeyi nahui metztli, zan otechmamauhtiaya.

140

Not a single federal soldier was left in the streets of Milpa Alta. By this time, Zapata's men had taken hold of the hill of the Teuhtli. The federals had fled towards San Gregorio and Xochimilco, not stopping until they reached Churubusco.

At that time, no one dreamed of the coming of Carranza's troops.

I was fourteen years old and was frightened—as were all the people of the village—by the gunfire. The Zapatistas were scattered about the hills of Teuhtli, Tijeras, and Ocpayoca. The federals were living in the village of Milpa Alta. These men were called federals at the time that Porfirio Díaz ruled.

So it was that from these three mountains the men of Zapata surrounded the federals. They chased them into the woods. Some fled towards San Pablo Oztotepec. They reached the mountain called Cuauhtzin. But there many Zapatistas had gathered. They were hidden among the hills. When they saw the federal soldiers going by, Zapata's men began to shoot. This was the end of the federals—and they were many. Three or four federal soldiers managed to get away. They reached Milpa Alta. And by that time a reinforcement had arrived from the Capital.

It was rumored in the village that Zapata's men were gathering again to provoke the federals. There was a lot of gunfire, and bullets were answered by bullets. Thus passed three or four months. They were only scaring us!

141

Opehque *carrancistas* oacito ompan toxolal. Occepa omocuecuepotzaque *carrancistas* ica *zapatistas*. Oquinchololtique *zapatistas* ica cuauhtla nochi otli Santa Ana ihuan San Lorenzo. Omoctaya quen tlapopoca ica ocholoayan. Amo tla oyeya mimiquez nian *carrancista* nian *zapatista*.

Ama omic. Zan yehuan chantlaca—inomequez cualcan yahue cuentla—inimequez oquinmictique. Cente tlachiquero ica inecua, cente xiuhcuique, cente cuacuahque: !yehuan on oquinquitzque miquiztli ipan otli!

Ihcuac omopeuh *carrancistas* neci mahuiztique. Tenonotzaya ihuan oquihuitequia caltemitl. Oquixohuaya ihuan otelhuiaya "Ihquin techpactia. Amo nancholozque. Ximo-

XVI. THE MEN OF THE NORTH

On the fifteenth of July, 1914, threatened by the armies of the North, by Zapata on the South, and by American forces in Veracruz, the dictator Huerta flees the country. Led by Obregón and Villa, thousands of northerners swarm over the southern part of the Republic. Mexico City falls into their hands. Zapata continues to control the part of Mexico immediately south of the Capital.

Almost two years pass. Milpa Alta and the mountain villages are finally taken on February 12, 1916, by the forces of the North. Several hundred men—some of them Yaquis and Mayos—enter the village.

If you only knew, professor, all the things that happened to us when Zapata abandoned us! The people of the village will never forgive him for leaving us in the hands of the enemy. Strangers began to arrive, men wearing earrings. One wore a large golden ring in his nose. They spoke Spanish, I think, but we could hardly understand a word they said. They spoke with thick, brutish accents. They were the men of Carranza!

When the Carrancistas invaded our lands, the shooting began again, this time between the men of Carranza and Zapata. Zapata's men were forced to flee into the woods, all the way up the path towards Santa Ana and San Lorenzo. Their flight was like a forest fire, but there were no dead on either side.

143

caltzacuacua. Itic namocal amotla namechpanoz." Ihuan amoca ocholo.

Inimequez *carrancistas* amo cualtin tique; oyeya coza tlacatecolotlaca. Nochi oquichihuaya. Techachan ocalaquia. Quimichtequia cuanacame, pitzome, tlacuali. Tla otlacualolotaya nochi tlacuali—tlaxcali, tepalcame—oquinhuicaya. Oncuan on chantlaca aihmo tlacuaya. Tla oquihtaya ce cuatemixalo ocanaya ihuan itic ipoxa ocaquiaya. Tla tlacatl nozo cihuatl ocuicaya achi cuali tzotzoma oquiquixtiliaya.

Ye yiman on oyahque ica cuauhtla in *zapatistas*. Oquincahque ipan xolal in *carrancistas*. Ican chicnahui tlapoali in yohuali otemoquen in *zapatistas* ihuan occepa oquinchololtique in *carrancistas*. Oacique ica San Gregorio Atlapulco, ica Xochimilco. Iqui on oyeque huecatica. Oyaya *carrancistas*, tlacuecuepotzaya; *zapatistas* otlananquiliaya noihqui otlacuecuepotzaya. Ce tonaltica ocalahque *carrancistas* ihuan *zapatistas* occepa ocholoque.

Inin tlaca icuac Carranza onene ihuan ompoyon oyeque *tropa de Amaro* itropa ihuan ompoyon oquipiaya ce *cuartel*. Amo ticmatizque tlica oquitlalilique inin otli Espinazo. Oquizaya inin otli ixitlancopa teuhtzin inin otli ihuan icuac omomomotlaya *carrancistas* ica *zapatistas*. Ipan in otli oquimacique in *soldados* cox huelez ahuelo tzicuinia; ican otlatlahuelcuitaya ipampa yoquimacia *zapatistas*. Oquitenehuaya inimequez *carrancistas*:"¡Ahueli titzicuinizque itech! Neci ce icuitlapanxiloyo xolopictli.

144

The only dead were the people of the village, those who had gotten up early to work in the fields. Those were the ones who died. A man who had gone to get aguamiel from his maguey plants, another who had gone to the woods to gather herbs, a wood-cutter—those were the ones whom death caught on the road!

At the beginning, these Carrancistas seemed to be nice men. They talked to the people of the village and knocked at the doors of the houses. When we came out, they would say, "That's the way we like it! Don't run away from the village. Stay in your houses. If you stay here, you will be safe." And no one ran away from the village.

But later we found out that the Carrancistas were owls. They were devils. They were capable of doing all sorts of evil things. They went into the houses. They stole our chickens, pigs, and food. If they caught us eating, they carried away all the food, together with the tortillas and dishes, leaving us without anything to eat. They would even grab a broken pot and stick it into their pockets. If a man or woman happened to be wearing good clothes, they were stripped on the spot.

It was then that the men of Zapata fled again to the mountains, leaving our lands in the hands of the Carrancistas. But at nine o'clock one night, the Zapatistas came down again and chased the Carrancistas out. The Carrancistas fled as far as San Gregorio Atlapulco and Xochimilco. They stayed there for some time. Carranza's men

Ihuan nian techacizque ihuan techmimictizque ipampa inin otli coza tlaixtli."

In *carrancistas* oquimoquixtiliaya tzotzomatli de teopantli ihuan omaquiaya yehuan. Icuac oquinequia motlaquitazque in tzotzomatli de teopantli, ohualaya in *milagro* ihuan omotepexihuiaya cuauhtlapechco in *carrancistas*. Occequintin oquinmotemohuiliaya in *santos* ica omahuiltiaya. Zan otlathuia yomic.

In *santo* nobarrio, inintzin teotl itocatzin San Mateo, omotehuitequiliaya can tecoco. Icuac *carrancistas* ocalahque noihqui mach quimoxinatlalilizque nochi tzotzomatli.

Ce tlacatl oicataya teopantli ihuan chantlaca. Noihqui ompa oyeya quitztoque tlen quichihuazque *carrancistas*.

"Inin tlacatecolotl *carrancista*," oquito chantlacatl tobarrio, "yotleco itlauhtzinco San Mateo. Quinequi maquiz icapatzin. ¡Noihqui itzotzomatzin San Marcos, iconetzin Mateo!"

Icuac oquicaque inin tlatoli chantlaca oquilhuique centetl: "¡Amo ximotequipacho! Ahueli tlaquimoquixtililizque San Mateo. Ahquen itechtzinco mayahuiz quimotlatzontequiliz."

"¿Quenin quimotlatzontequilililiz?" Oquito ce *carrancista*: "¿Quenin quimomaguiliz nozo quimocueponiliz?"

"Namechmomaquiliz cente cocoliztli itoca atonahuiztli," oquimilhuique chantlacatl. "Nian nican namotzonteco nanenemizque ihuan amo nancehuizque. ¡Achi milagrosotzin!"

Ihuan inin ce *carrancista* oquitemohuic *capa de* San

146

would attack the village, and those of Zapata fought back with many bullets.

Carranza and the troops of Amaro kept their headquarters in Milpa Alta. One of the streets got to be nicknamed "The Backbone of the Devil." This street lay in the direction of the Teuhtli, where the men of Carranza and Zapata fought. The soldiers of Carranza became weary of running. They were sometimes caught along this road. They were frightened to death because they could see the Zapatistas catching up with them. "We cannot run up here!" they cried. "It looks like the spine of the devil himself! Here they will catch us and kill us on this devilish road."

The men of Carranza stole vestments from the churches of the village and dressed up in them. Once they had put on the holy robes, they suffered accidents and fell off the altars. Others pulled the images of the saints down from the altars to play around with them. But the next morning, the Carrancistas were found dead.

The saint who watched over my quarter was called San Mateo and an angry saint he was! When the Carrancistas entered the village, they boasted that they would strip him of his robes.

One day a man from our district of San Mateo of Milpa Alta was standing in the church with other men of the village, waiting to see what the Carrancistas would do.

"This dirty Carrancista!" the man from our district said. "He has climbed up to the altar where San Mateo stands.

Mateo. Opeuh quicocototza ihuan zan niman opeuh huehueyoca. In oc centetl *carrancista* tlaxitla oyeya quimol-
huilia: "¡Nehuatl amotla nimitzchihuilia Mateo! ¡Nian
amo nicocotoza motzotzoma! Ica on huel miac nimitztla-
tlauhtia, amo tinechmacaz atonahuiztli. Nehuatl noneltoca
ica coza timilagroso. Amo oquinequia noneltocaz. Axcan
nixpan pano ica nixtelolohuan oniquictac quenin otihuite-
quilic cocoliztli in nomaiuhniuh *carrancista*. Inon otiqui-
macac atonahuiztli."

Ohuecauh cana caxtoli tonali cocoxqui. Huehueyoca
ihuan amotla oquichihuiliaya tlapatli. Ica ipan *guerra*
oyeya tepatiquez amo tepatique. Ica in omic *carrancista*.

Oyec tonali ce *carrancista* oquinequia quimotemo-
huilizque tonantzin La Asunción. Quintzatzilia occequi
tlaca oncuanon quipalehuizque quinmotemohuilizque
tonantzin. Yehuatzin motlaixotilia ipan toxolal ihuan
huecapa metztica. Ihcuac tla ilhuitl quinmotemohuilia
cana cempoali tlaca ihuan quinmolpilia ica nelpilontin
chichicatiquez; oncuanon amo tlatzcotoni. Ihuan in *carrancistas* oquitoque "Tictemohuizque inin xenola, tiquix-
tilizque in *corona*, pipiloltin ihuan itzotzoma." Amo ipan
omomatia tla yeticatzintli in tonantzin.

Zan ce *carrancista* otlecoc huan oquimomatoquili ye
ticatzintli. Oquintzatzili occequintin. Otlecoque nahui
ihuan yehuatl ye macuiltin. Mach quimoxinacatlalilizque
in Tonantzin. Ye oquicxicahque *altar* ihuan omotepexihui-
que. Cente omopepetoni icxi; occente opoztec iman ihuan
inon achton otlecoc oxixiticac itzonteco.

148

He wants to put on the saint's mantle! And the robes of San Marcos, too, the robes of the son of Mateo!"

When they heard these words, the men of the village spoke up. "Do not worry. No one can take anything away from San Mateo. He who dares to touch him will be killed."

"How can he slay us?" one of the men of Carranza asked. "How can he beat us up or shoot us with bullets?"

"You are going to get sick with a sickness called fever," the men of the village said. "And you won't be able to get rid of it, even if you tried walking on your head! For our San Mateo is a terrible saint!"

But the Carrancista took the mantle of San Mateo and brought it down with him from the altar. He tore the cape to bits, and then he began to shake with the fever.

The other soldier who had been standing below cried, "Oh, Mateo, I am not doing you any harm! Nor am I tearing your clothes! I beg you not to send me the fever. Only now do I realize that you are an angry saint, a saint who hits hard. I did not want to believe this. But now I have seen how you struck my fellow Carrancista with fever!"

The sick man lived about two weeks. He shook all over, and no medicine helped him. Because those were times of war, our witch doctors would not attend him. So it was that this soldier of Carranza died.

The day came when a certain Carrancista decided to bring down from her altar the image of Our Mother, Our Lady of the Assumption, the patroness of our village. He

149

Tle oquitaque ihuan occequi oquinonotzque tlen ipampa omococoque ihuan occequi omopepetotzque. Ica in
aihmo ce tonali tla oquichiuhque ocalaquia teopan ihuan
omotlancuaquetzaya omoteochihuaya.

Occequi *carrancistas* oquinequia oquicuepque teopantli
cahuacorral ihuan oquincalaque cahuatin itic teopantli.
Ican yopapano tlemach intlac occequi tlanonotzaya. "Amo
xiquincalaquica itic teocali; cuache tla namechpanoz."
Zan niman ooquinquixtique cahuatin. Ipan *cementerio*
ompoyon oyeya: oquicuepque cahuacorral.

called the other soldiers to help him bring Our Mother down. She cares for our village and stands on high. When there is a fiesta, twenty men take her image down and always bind her with strong woven bands to a wooden platform. That is the way she is taken out on a procession.

But the men of Carranza said, "We will bring this woman down. We will strip her of her crown, her earrings and her robes!" They did not know that Our Mother was so heavy.

One of Carranza's men climbed up above the altar and then he realized that she was heavy. He called others to help him. Four men climbed up the altar, so that now there were five. They were going to undress Our Mother! But they tripped on the altar and came rolling down. One hurt his foot, another broke his arms, and the one who had climbed up first bashed his head in.

Those who saw these happenings told others the reason why the soldiers of Carranza got sick and why they broke their bones. From this time on, they stopped doing evil things within the church. And from this time on, they would kneel down to pray.

Other Carrancistas wanted to turn the church into a stable and to keep their horses in the church. But because of the things that had happened, others told them, "Don't keep them in the church! Terrible things may happen to you." And so, the horses were left in the church yard. This, they turned into a stable.

151

Ye yiman tica in oquimoquitzquilique teopixque. Omo-
tlatitzinotaya ipan cente cali ihuan oquimoquixtilique.
Otlanonontzaloya quename ce tlatihuani tepatique itocatzin Basurto cuali oquimixmachiliaya topixque ipampa
ompa huecauh omochantili. Omotelhuilic: "¡Xiquitzqui-
can in topixque!"

Iquin oquimochihuili topixqui: oquimoquitzquilique,
oquimoxotlatlapachilique ixohpaltzitzihuan ihuan oqui-
monenemitilique in topixque.

152

XVII. THE FATE OF THE PRIEST

The government of Mexico City accuses the clergy of being allies of Zapata. The parish priests of the villages of Tulyehualco and Iztapalapa, together with the curate of San Antonio Tomatlan, are jailed in Mexico City. Their parishioners fight in vain to free them.

Father Polo of Milpa Alta is also arrested.

It was about this time that the priest was caught. He had been hiding in one of the homes, and they dragged him out. It was rumored that the doctor by the name of Basurto knew the priest well, since the doctor had lived in Milpa Alta for a long time. But now he joined the Carrancistas and said, "Get the priest!"

And this is what they did to the priest. They caught him. They slit open the soles of his feet. And then they forced him to walk that way.

Oquimatque *zapatistas* tlen oquimaitilique topixque ihuan ahquen otlatequihti. Occepa ohualtemoque *zapatistas* ihuan oquimiquilique topixque; oquitequixtilique itlalpan. Ayoquic omomachix tla omomiquili nozo monemiti.

Ican yocalaque *carrancistas* yomochantlalique, omitoaya ayoquic hualazque *zapatistas*.

Nehuatl oninamacaya atoli ihuan nacatamali tianquizco. Ihuan ce tonaltica ohualtemoque *zapatistas* ica Texetaco otli. Oquixtetzico occequi ica Tecpampa otli. Ce *vuelta* otlacuecuepotzaque *zapatistas* ihuan otzatzique: "¡Nemi Zapata! ¡Nemi Zapata! Nian ca namotata; ayemo miqui. ¡Nemi Zapata!"

Ihuan *carrancistas* otlayitaya itenco acaxtontli itentla tianquiztli, icuac otiquimictaque huaquetztaque. Ah

154

XVIII. ZAPATA IS STILL ALIVE

But Zapata returns to rescue the priest.

The men of Zapata found out what had been done to the priest and who had given the orders. Again the Zapatistas came down and they saved the priest. They carried him back to their lands. We never found out whether the priest died or survived.

Since the soldiers of Carranza had established their barracks in Milpa Alta, it was thought that the Zapatistas would never return.

One day, while I was selling *atole* and meat tamales in the square the men of Zapata came rushing down the street called Texetaco. Others entered the town down the street of Tecpampa. Suddenly they began to shoot and yell, "Zapata is alive! Zapata is alive! Your father is here. He is not dead! Zapata is alive!"

quimatiz tlica huaquetztaque. Zan niman tzatzi itic tianquiztli *zapatistas*: "¡Nian ca namotata! ¡Ayemo miqui!"
Ihuan tehuan ototohtiaya *pilastras* tianquiztli. Iqui on amo
techaxiliz tepoztlacueponali.
    Ye yiman oquizque *zapatistas*; otlecoque occepa ica
cuauhtla. Achi miaque *carrancistas* omihque. Ye yiman on
occepa omachix ica yoyahque *zapatistas* ica Tepoztlan,
Yautepec ihuan Cuauhnahuac. Ompoyon quezqui tonali
aihmo omocuepque; aihmo tlamictizque. Ohuecauh oacico occepa *zapatistas*. Omonamihque cuauhtlanepantla
zapatistas ican *carrancistas*. Ompoyon omomomimihtique.
Ye yiman on otlecoque *carrancistas hasta* ica Cuauhnahuac. Occepa ompoyon oquimimictique *carrancistas*.
Ihuan cihuame ihuan tlaca *en* Cuauhnahuac onecaltza-
cualoya. Huan ipan otli yan omocuecuepotzaya. [. . .]

Several of the Carrancista soldiers were eating breakfast on the edge of the stone fountain near the market place. Suddenly, we saw them fall flat on their backs. No one knew why they had fallen. Then the men of Zapata came shouting into the market place, "Your father has arrived! Zapata is not dead!" And we girls held on to the columns of the market and hid behind them. In this way, we were saved from a stray bullet.

Then the Zapatistas went away again. They fled toward the woods. But many Carrancistas had been slain. We found out that the Zapatistas had taken the road to Tepoztlan, Yautepec, and Cuernavaca. They did not return for some days. They did not come back to kill. It was a long time before the men of Zapata returned.

The Zapatistas and Carrancistas met in the middle of the wilderness. And there they killed one another. At one time, the Carrancistas got as far as Cuernavaca, and many of them died there. The women and men of Cuernavaca would lock themselves up in their homes. There was a lot of shooting in the streets. But we never heard about our Father Polo again!

Ye yiman tica on ce tonaltica *carrancistas* oquinquix-
tique in chachantzinco tlaca-pipiltototon queman caxtol-
xiuhca yomen occequin matlactli ihuan ome ihuan yeyi
xihuitl oquipiaya, cocoltin, telpocame, chichicahuazque
tlaca-ihuan oquinmimictique nochtin ipan tianquiztli.
    Oquinmoquixtilito inchachantzinco nochtintzitzin tla-
came. Amotla omocalactiaya. Iman tica on oquinmomic-
tilique notatzin, notiotzitzihuan. Cetzin notiotzin chicah-
que tlatihuani ihuan occetzin ye tocoltzin. Yomomiquili-
taya icuac ocalaque calitic *carrancistas* ihuan inintzin coli
oquinmanalique ican tlali oquimomochilique.
    Oquinquixtique queman chicuacen tlapoali huatzin-
copa. Zan cecpa oquitlacalque ce *metralladora*. Ica on
oquimimictique.

XIX. THE MASSACRE

The people of Milpa Alta have shown their hatred toward the government in Mexico City. Milpa Alta is the strategic point between the National Palace and the lairs of Zapata in Morelos. Peace cannot come to Mexico until the Zapatista guerrillas are eliminated.

One morning at dawn the tecolotl—*the owl of death of the Indian world—comes to perch upon the steeple of the church and watch.*

And one day the men of Carranza dragged the men from their houses—the fifteen-year-old boys, those of twelve or thirteen, the old, the young, the strong—and they killed them all in the village square before the church.

They dragged all the men from their houses. Our men had not meddled at all with politics. They killed my father and my uncles. One of my uncles was a strong man, and the other was a little old man. He was already dying when the men of Carranza entered his house and grabbed the old one and smashed him against the earth floor.

They took all of them out at about six in the morning. Only one blast echoed from the machine gun. Thus they were slain.

Pigs and dogs fed upon the dead.

Pitzome, chichime, oquincuaya mimiquez.
Nochayauhtaya cemilhuitl ihuan cen yohuali. [. . .]
[. . .] Cihuame ihuan ichpocatoton Momochco oquin-
tocaque mimiquez zancualcantica. Cihuame otlaltata-
caque can quintocazque inamic huan nozo ipilhuan. Ican
tlacayo oquinmomimictilique ipan ce tecochtli oquinten-
que chicueyi nozo matlactli mimiquez ihuan oquintlal-
pachoaya. Icihcan, cuache pehuazque mocuecuepotzaz-
que occepa tlacatecolotlaca.

Ce tonaltica amo molinique nian *zapatistas* nian *carrancistas*. Otecahque ma motocacan mimiquez.

Zan macuili tlacatl opolihuia cano acini omecientos
mimiquez.

Yoquimomictilique notatzin ihuan ye yiman on nonantzin huel omochoquiliaya. Topan ocalaque in *carrancistas*
ihuan zan oquinmocemixohtilique. Nonantzin omopiliaya
ya colpatzinco ce *ceñidor* iyaxcatzin notatzin.

"¿Tlica tichoca?" tlatlani in *carrancista*. "¿Ican oquimi-
tique monamic? Xinechmaca *ceñidor*; noihqui icoton
monamic naquiz. Tla amo tinechmacaz nimitzmictiz."

Omonequilti ihuan amo, nonantzin omotemaquili. Iqui
on oquichiuhtinemia techachan in *carrancistas*.

Icuac *zapatistas* otlecoque ica Tepoztlan achi miaque
zapatistas omique ipan ce xolal itocayoca Amantlan.
Oquinmimictique *zapatistas*; ompoyon omic cente *general*
itoca Marcelino Muñoz ihuan occe itoca Reyes Muñoz.

Ihuan ohualtemoque in *carrancistas* ica itzonteco in

160

There lay the dead for a whole day and a night. None of the women knew what had happened. We remained enclosed in our houses. But the following dawn, the little old women came out, crawling through the streets, afraid of being shot down. And there in front of the church we saw my uncle with his guts pulled out. The dogs had pulled them out.

With the hoes and machetes of the men, all the women and girls of Milpa Alta scraped out pits in the churchyard to bury their husbands, fathers, and sons. But there were so many men killed, the women threw eight or ten bodies in each pit and covered them with earth. Fast, before the human devils—the owls—began to fight again.

For a whole day, neither the men of Carranza or Zapata moved. They permitted the dead to be buried.

They had already killed my father, and my mother was crying hard. Carranza's men entered the house and stared at her. On her shoulder, my mother was wearing a sash which had belonged to my father.

"Why are you crying?" one of the Carrancistas asked her. "Because they killed your husband? Give me the sash. And I am also going to put on your husband's serape. If you don't give it to me, I will kill you!"

Whether she wanted to or not, my mother gave them to him. So went the men of Carranza from house to house.

When Zapata's men went down toward Tepoztlan, many of them died in the town called Amantla. They killed

matech ocualicayan. Oquinquechcotonqui. In matech tzontecomatl in Reyes Muñoz ihuan otlatlania: "¿Ahquen quixmati itzonteco inin tlacatl?" Ayahca onahuat. Nochtlacatl oquixmatia amaca onahuat ipampa cuache temimictizque *carrancistas*.

Zapata's men. A general named Marcelino Muñoz and another named Reyes Muñoz also died there.

And the men of Carranza came down into Milpa Alta with the head of Reyes Muñoz in their hands. They had cut off his head. They were carrying the head of Reyes Muñoz and were asking, "Who recognizes the head of this man?" Nobody answered because the men of Carranza would come to kill again.

163

Ye yiman tica on otetemohuique *carrancistas* ica metztli julio. Otechcuito huan otechilhuique: "Icihcan nanquizazque denamochan. Tla amo nanquinequi nanquizazque, quitoznequi quename nanquintlazotla in *zapatistas*. ¡Ihuan hualazque tlamimihtizque tohuazcahuan!"

Ye yiman opapanoc cana yeyi nozo nahui metztli. Ipan chicueyi metztli *de* notlan otlamimihtito otechilhui *carrancista*: "Tla amo nanyazque ica Mexico titliquechizque nochtin caltin." Otechcuito ihuan otechcahque Mexico. Cequintin tlaca onecahualo ica San Gregorio Atlapulco; occequi hualaque ican Xochimilco, ca otlaixmatia.

Icuac *carrancistas* oyahque techcuito otehualicaque tlaca *hasta* Xochimilco ihuan ipan *cementerio* otecalaquique. Tlen otihualaque ica yohuali otiquizque Momochco

164

XX. FLIGHT

Though most of the men of the village are dead, Mexico City considers that Milpa Alta is still dangerous to the government. The survivors of the massacre, almost all women and children, are forced to leave the village.

Then in the month of July the Carrancistas came again. They came to turn us out. They said, "You will have to leave your homes soon. And if you refuse to leave, that means that you are on the side of Zapata. Then our men will come to kill you!"

Then three or four months went by. In the eighth month after the massacre the men of Carranza told us, "Either you go away to Mexico City or we will burn down all the houses!" They seized us all and took us away to Mexico City. Some stayed behind in San Gregorio Atlapulco. Others went to Xochimilco where they knew some people.

When the Carrancistas expelled us, they brought the people as far as Xochimilco and shut them up in the cemetery. But some of us, those who came by night, left Milpa

Malacateticpac queman chicnahui nozo matlactli tlatepoz-
machotiloni. Nochtin tlen otihualaque ica yohuali otihual-
momamacaya tlaoli, yetzintli, ahuax ihuan itic xinachtli
noihqui omoten tepitzin tomin. Ihuan occequi ipan one-
cuitlalpilo. Oncuan on tla tlaotequixtiliani yetzintli nozo
tlaoli amo nochi otequixtiliani.

Onetequipacholoya ipampa amoca oteixmatia ica Mexico ca occequi *lugar*. Ihuan iqui on omonemili oncuan ica
panozque tepilhuan ihuan tatatin amo motequipachozque
ica tomin. Ica on oyohualquixohuac. Amatlacauhcualicac
nian chichi, nian miztli, nian ce cuanaca cuache chiquelet-
zatzin ihuan quicaquizque in *carrancistas*.

Iqui on otihualtemoque ca icpac Tehhuehuentin. Oquitz-
quizaco ica San Luis Acuezcomatl. Yompoyon onexexe-
lolo cequi tlacatl. Cequi ohualhuiloac *hasta* San Gregorio
Atlapulco. Tlen yotlaixmatia ica Xochimilco ohualaque
onetlalilo tlanamaco.

Alta at about nine or ten o'clock. We who came by night carried corn, beans, lima beans—and among these seeds were scattered a few coins. Others had coins hidden in their sashes. In this way, if the corn and beans were taken from them, they had not lost all.

The hearts of the people were troubled because they knew no one in Mexico City nor in any other place. They had but one thought—that of keeping their children and fathers and mothers alive without starving for need of money. That is why they fled the village at night. No one carried a dog or a cat or a hen which might cackle and give them away to the Carrancistas.

Thus it was that we descended by the Teuhtli. Some people came through San Luis Acuezcomatl. Some stayed behind at that place. Others got as far as San Gregorio Atlapulco. Those who knew people in Xochimilco remained there and made a living buying and selling.

Omocencuic tlaoli; occequi tlacatl oquicencuia cuauh-
itl ihuan omonamacaya. Iqui on ica onepalehuiloya
oncuan amo tlamiz icihcan tomin, noca ca quinextiz
tequitl. Occequintin cihuame oquimanaya tlaxcali ihuan
ocuicaya tianquiztli Xochimilco quinamacazque. Ipan tica
on tonaltin coza otlanamacoya. Occequi oquitlalique tlacuali, noihqui oncuan monamacaz: atoli, tamali. Ye
yiman tica on coza oyaya Mexico caxtilteca Xochimilco
ihuan coza otlanamacoya. Iqui on quen onepalehuiloya
noca onextequitl *para* tlaca.

Noihqui ichpocame oquintlaquehuaya metztequitizque.
Ican amo oquimatia que nemoa Mexico mexicatlaca,
oquintlaxtlahuiaya achi tepiltzin. Amo quen axan, metzte-

168

XXI. THE STRUGGLE FOR LIFE

The homeless exiles find ways of making a living in Xochimilco and Mexico City, but the struggle for survival is not easy.

Some people traded in corn. Others went out to gather firewood to sell. Thus they supported themselves in order not to run out of money until they found work. Some of the women made tortillas and went to sell them in the market place of Xochimilco. Much was sold there in those times. Others made food—atole and tamales—also to be sold. Many Spanish-speaking people from Mexico City would go to Xochimilco in those times. So did our people manage to survive until they found work.

Some of the girls also took jobs as servants. But because they were not used to the way of life in Mexico City, the people paid them very little. They were not like maids of today who make a lot of money. Those girls were paid

169

quitzquez quitlani hueyi tomin. Inimequez ichpocame zan
oquintlaxtlahuiaya macuili *peso* cana matlactli. Ompoyon
amo panoaya tlaxtlahuili.

Tlacayo ocalacoac oncuan Mexico; noihqui otlanama-
caya, Occequi opantlacencuia. Occequi oquicencuia cuahuitl; oquixexeloaya ihuan icaltempa oquinamacaya.

Cihuapili itocatzin Tomasita oquimopiliaya ce pipiltontli itocan Conchito. Tzitziquitzin omocauh icnoton
ipampa oquimomictilique itatzin. Inin cihuapili amo
omomachtiaya caxtilan tlatoli ihuan ohualmicac Mexico.
Omocecuili pantzin ihuan omotlalitzin ixpan ce cini.
Omotelhuiliaya: "¡Nicnamaca cocoliztli!" Cana yexpa
omotenehuiliaya. Huan cihuame tlen oquimixmachiliaya
ihuan quimatia caxtilancopa oquimolhuilique: "Tomasita,
aihmo ximitalhui 'Nicnamaca cocoliztli.' Ximitalhui
'Nicnamaca cocoles.' Ihuan timotiliz ica timotlanama-
quiliz."

170

about five or ten pesos a month. They never made more than that.

Many of the people also came into the city to sell things. Some brought bread to sell. Others gathered firewood. They split it and sold it on the sidewalk in front of the houses in which they lived.

A woman by the name of Tomasita had a little boy called Conchito. He had been an orphan since he was a baby because his father had been killed in the massacre. Without knowing how to speak Spanish, this woman came to the Capital. She bought some breads and sat down in front of a movie house and tried to sell them. "I sell *cocoliztli* (sickness)!" she cried. She yelled this three times. But the women who were her friends and who knew Spanish said to her "Tomasita, stop saying 'I sell sickness!' Say, 'I sell bread (*cocoles*),' and you will see how well it sells!"

Icuac ohuiloac ica tlaxitla—ma tiquitocan ica Cuauhnahuac—acique ipan ce tepetl itoca tepetl Jilguero. Ompoyon oquitlaliz Zapata iestacamento. Ican yoquimatia
yauh tlapoloz amo ica on omotecuicho, *sino* oquimilhuic
isoldadohuan.

"¡Nanechtoca," oquito Zapata, "*hasta* campa tlamiz
último cartucho! Ihuan tla nechmictia xicayan namehuan.
Macamo namechquitziquican Everardo González huan
Andrés Campos ica Melchor Campos. Ihuan tla amo
nanequizque nanechtocazque, xicayan intlal Tierra Fría.
¡Aihmo xinechtocacan! Nian ca tlen nanquicuazque ipan
otli. Xicalaquican ompa Mexico. ¡Amotla namechpanoz!"

Achtocopa *de* inin oquimaciqui *zapatistas* ipan *llano*

XXII. TILL THE LAST CARTRIDGE
IS GONE

In April, 1919, rumors circulate among the refugees in Xochi-milco and Mexico City. Zapata is dead! Let us hear our informant's version of the assassination.

When the Zapatistas went away in the direction of Cuernavaca, they reached a mountain known as the Cerro del Jilguero. It was there that Zapata set up his camp. And though he knew he was going to lose, his spirit did not fail him. He spoke to his soldiers.

"Follow me," Zapata said, "until the last cartridge is gone! And if they kill me, go away. Let not the lives of Everardo González, of Andrés Campos and Melchor Campos be lost! And if you do not want to follow me, go up to the highlands and abandon me. Here is enough money for you to live on the road. Go to México City. Nothing bad will happen to you there."

Before this, the Zapatistas had been caught on the plains

Salazar. Ompoyon oquinmehualoque oncanon ahueli quizazque.

Ce cihuatontli itoca Francisca González Chávez, notia ichan San Lorenzo Tlacoyuca tlacpac Momochco Malacatepec, ohuiloac Salazar. Yoquimictique *carrancistas* inamic ihuan yehuatl amo cana omomauhti quintoca *zapatistas* ipan on *llano* Salazar. Aih hueli ca ocholo. Inin cihuatzintli oquitzonhuique ica ce *riata*: icihcan oquitecaxquixti *riata* inin techicocoh. Ye yiman on ocholoc ohuala Mexico.

Iman ohualaque inimequez Tierra Fría *soldados* oquicahque Zapata ipan tepetl Jilguero huan tlanonotzaloque oquicuamanque Zapata. Oyac inin *general* itocan Amaro huan oquicuaman Zapata. Oquito: "Ye niguala ononeloco namotlac. Aihmo nicarrancista ¡axcan ye nizapatista!"

Zapata zazan *confiado*. Oquineltocac Amaro ihuan oquitlali itlac quename melahuac isoldado. Ihuan niman Amaro oquimictic in Zapata.

174

of Salazar. They were surrounded there, with no means of escape.

A lady by the name of Francisca González Chávez, my aunt, from San Lorenzo Tlacoyuca above Milpa Alta, went to Salazar. The Carrancistas had already killed her husband, and she was not afraid of following the men of Zapata to the plains of Salazar even though no one could escape from there. And there she was lassoed by an enemy rope. But quickly she managed to free herself from the noose which held her around the neck. So it was that she fled towards Mexico City.

When his soldiers went away to the highlands, they left Zapata alone at the Cerro del Jilguero. It is said that a trap was set for him. A general by the name of Amaro was the one who betrayed Zapata. "I have come to join you," he said. "I am no longer with Carranza! I am with Zapata now!"

Zapata trusted him. He believed Amaro, who joined the army as if he had been one of Zapata's soldiers. It was then that Amaro killed Zapata.

Icuac oticholoque ihuan ocholoque *zapatistas* toxolal omocauh icel Momochco Malacatepec. Omocauhque cuanacame, chichime, mimiztin, pitzome, cahuatin. Ican ahuel otiquinmamaque Mexico ompa otiquincahque.

Oticuepaloco cana ipan nahui xihuitl ompa ipan toxolal. Nochtlacatl ohuiloac ica teyolo, [. . .] moctaz tlen tehuaxca: tlaltin, xolaltin, caltin.

Ohuaxihuac ipan xolaltin. ¡Miltin quename cuauhtlatli yomochiuh! Ohuepahque achi miaque cuauhtin: axtlacapalcuauhtin, tecapulcuahuitl huan capulcuauhtin. Achi miaque omochiuhque. Achton ohuiloac otlanonotzaloya quename itech cuauhtin omotampiloaya cocoa. Icuac on onechantiloto omotlatlacalque cuauhtin. Iqui on ica

XXIII. THE RETURN TO MILPA ALTA

The exiles return to Milpa Alta with heavy hearts.

When we fled and when the men of Zapata abandoned our lands, not a soul was left in Milpa Alta. But chickens were left behind, and dogs and pigs and horses. Because we could not take them with us to Mexico City, we left them there.

About four years later, we returned to our village. With courageous hearts the people went back to see what had been their possessions—lands, cornfields, houses.

They arrived in the village. The cornfields had become forests! Trees had grown, tepozanes, willows, and wild cherry trees! Trees were everywhere! The men and women who went back first all spoke of the snakes which hung from the tree branches. When they went back to live there,

occepa onemoaloton. Cana yeyi, nahui xiuhpa ocuache ye tlacayo ohuiloac ompa.

Achtocopa zan huehueca caltin oyeya, ihuan otlama-mauhtiloaya ica occepa. "¡Ye huitze *zapatistas!*" nozo "¡Ye huitze *carrancistas!*" Yotlan.

[. . .] Ihuan noihqui ipan yohuali tlamamauhtiloli: cente tlacatl ihuan ce cihuatl tepan otechachancalaquia. Zan oransio yonetetepacholo.

Ihuan occepa tequiti axcan tlacame momochco. Quim-pia tepilhuan: *licenciados*, temachtiquez, totopixque. Yoixtlapouhque.

Nican yotlan notlatol ipan Momochco Malacateticpac, altepetl tepetzalan, Teuhtli ihuan Cuauhtzin, intzalan Mexico ihuan Tepoztlan.

they cut down the trees. In this way the village was inhabited again. After three or four years, more people went back to live there again.

Before our return, our homes had been scattered, apart from each other, and the inhabitants were always frightened by cries of "The Zapatistas are coming!" or "The Carrancistas are coming!" But those days are gone.

It seems that two ghosts had felt free to roam about in the ruins of the houses of the village we had deserted. They made their homes there. They went from house to house, sometimes entering one, sometimes another. When we returned, the phantoms became confused and did not know which house to stay in. So it was that they haunted our houses at night. They were a man and a woman. They had found a way into our homes. At about seven o'clock in the evening, every man would shut tight the door of his house.

But today, the people of my village are working again. They have sons—lawyers, professors, and priests. Their eyes are wide open now.

Here ends my story about Milpa Alta, the village between the mountains, between Teuhtli and Cuauhtzin, between Mexico City and Tepoztlan.

179

GLOSSARY

Aguamiel: The unfermented juice of the century plant.
Ajusco: A mountain range separating the Valley of Mexico from Morelos.
Atole: A porridge made of corn flour.
Barrio: A section, district, or ward of a town.
Cocol: A type of wheat bread.
Cuartillo: A dry measure equal to about one liter.
Cuauhtzin: A volcanic peak south of Milpa Alta.
Cuernavaca: A city to the south of Milpa Alta, capital of Morelos in the Hot Country.
Diana: A melody played by a brass band at festive occasions.
Epazote: A strong-smelling herb commonly used in Mexican dishes.
Iztaccihuatl: "The White Woman," a snow-covered volcanic mountain range east of Milpa Alta.

Maguey: The century plant.

Mayordomo: A village official in charge of a religious festival.

Mole: A chile sauce.

Nahuatl: The Aztec language.

Nanacatl: Mushroom.

Ocote: A resinous tree of the coniferous order.

Otomí: An Indian group living west and north of the Valley of Mexico.

Popocatepetl: "The Smoking Mountain," a great snow-covered volcano to the southeast of Milpa Alta.

Pulque: A light alcoholic drink; the fermented juice of the century plant.

Quechquemitl: A woman's garment, worn over the shoulders.

Rebozo: The native shawl or head covering.

Salvero: A village official with religious duties.

Tamal: A type of maize bread steamed in corn leaves.

Tecolotl: Owl.

Teporingo: A small mammal, similar to the rabbit.

Tepozan: A native tree with medicinal uses.

Tepoztlan: A village in the State of Morelos, south of Milpa Alta.

Teuhtli: A volcanic hill north of Milpa Alta; the sacred hill of the village.

Tortilla: A thin unleavened bread, shaped like a pancake.

Zapotec: An Indian group in the State of Oaxaca.

THE CIVILIZATION OF THE AMERICAN INDIAN SERIES

of which *Life and Death in Milpa Alta* is Volume 117, was inaugurated in 1932 by the University of Oklahoma Press, and has as its purpose the reconstruction of American Indian civilization by presenting aboriginal, historical, and contemporary Indian life. The following list is complete as of the date of publication of this volume.

1. *Forgotten Frontiers:* A Study of the Spanish Indian Policy of Don Juan Bautista de Anza, Governor of New Mexico, 1777–1787. Translated and edited by Alfred Barnaby Thomas.
2. Grant Foreman. *Indian Removal:* The Emigration of the Five Civilized Tribes of Indians.
3. John Joseph Mathews. *Wah'Kon-Tah:* The Osage and the White Man's Road.
4. Grant Foreman. *Advancing the Frontier, 1830–1860.*
5. John H. Seger. *Early Days Among the Cheyenne and Arapahoe Indians.* Edited by Stanley Vestal. Out of print.
6. Angie Debo. *The Rise and Fall of the Choctaw Republic.*
7. Stanley Vestal. *New Sources of Indian History, 1850–1891:* A Miscellany. Out of print.
8. Grant Foreman. *The Five Civilized Tribes.*
9. *After Coronado:* Spanish Exploration Northeast of New Mexico, 1696–1727. Translated and edited by Alfred Barnaby Thomas.
10. Frank G. Speck. *Naskapi:* The Savage Hunters of the Labrador Peninsula. Out of print.
11. Elaine Goodale Eastman. *Pratt:* The Red Man's Moses. Out of print.
12. Althea Bass. *Cherokee Messenger:* A Life of Samuel Austin Worcester.
13. Thomas Wildcat Alford. *Civilization.* As told to Florence Drake. Out of print.
14. Grant Foreman. *Indians and Pioneers:* The Story of the American Southwest Before 1830.
15. George E. Hyde. *Red Cloud's Folk:* A History of the Oglala Sioux Indians.
16. Grant Foreman. *Sequoyah.*
17. Morris L. Wardell. *A Political History of the Cherokee Nation, 1838–1907.* Out of print.
18. John Walton Caughey. *McGillivray of the Creeks.*
19. Edward Everett Dale and Gaston Litton. *Cherokee Cavaliers:* Forty Years of Cherokee History as Told in the Correspondence of the Ridge-Watie-Boudinot Family.
20. Ralph Henry Gabriel. *Elias Boudinot, Cherokee, and His America.* Out of print.

183

21. Karl N. Llewellyn and E. Adamson Hoebel. *The Cheyenne Way:* Conflict and Case Law in Primitive Jurisprudence.
22. Angie Debo. *The Road to Disappearance.*
23. Oliver La Farge and others. *The Changing Indian.* Out of print.
24. Carolyn Thomas Foreman. *Indians Abroad.* Out of print.
25. John Adair. *The Navajo and Pueblo Silversmiths.*
26. Alice Marriott. *The Ten Grandmothers.*
27. Alice Marriott. *María:* The Potter of San Ildefonso.
28. Edward Everett Dale. *The Indians of the Southwest:* A Century of Development Under the United States. Out of print.
29. *Popol Vuh:* The Sacred Book of the Ancient Quiché Maya. English version by Delia Goetz and Sylvanus G. Morley from the translation of Adrián Recinos.
30. Walter Collins O'Kane. *Sun in the Sky.*
31. Stanley A. Stubbs. *Bird's-Eye View of the Pueblos.* Out of print.
32. Katharine C. Turner. *Red Men Calling on the Great White Father.*
33. Muriel H. Wright. *A Guide to the Indian Tribes of Oklahoma.*
34. Ernest Wallace and E. Adamson Hoebel. *The Comanches:* Lords of the South Plains.
35. Walter Collins O'Kane. *The Hopis:* Portrait of a Desert People.
36. *The Sacred Pipe:* Black Elk's Account of the Seven Rites of the Oglala Sioux. Edited by Joseph Epes Brown.
37. *The Annals of the Cakchiquels,* translated from the Cakchiquel Maya by Adrián Recinos and Delia Goetz, with *Title of the Lords of Totonicapán,* translated from the Quiché text into Spanish by Dionisio José Chonay, English version by Delia Goetz.
38. R. S. Cotterill. *The Southern Indians:* The Story of the Civilized Tribes Before Removal.
39. J. Eric S. Thompson. *The Rise and Fall of Maya Civilization.* (Revised Edition).
40. Robert Emmitt. *The Last War Trail:* The Utes and the Settlement of Colorado. Out of print.
41. Frank Gilbert Roe. *The Indian and the Horse.*
42. Francis Haines. *The Nez Percés:* Tribesmen of the Columbia Plateau. Out of print.
43. Ruth M. Underhill. *The Navajos.*
44. George Bird Grinnell. *The Fighting Cheyennes.*
45. George E. Hyde. *A Sioux Chronicle.* Out of print.
46. Stanley Vestal. *Sitting Bull, Champion of the Sioux:* A Biography.
47. Edwin C. McReynolds. *The Seminoles.*
48. William T. Hagan. *The Sac and Fox Indians.*

184

49. John C. Ewers. *The Blackfeet:* Raiders on the Northwestern Plains.
50. Alfonso Caso. *The Aztecs:* People of the Sun. Translated by Lowell Dunham.
51. C. L. Sonnichsen. *The Mescalero Apaches.*
52. Keith A. Murray. *The Modocs and Their War.*
53. *The Incas of Pedro de Cieza de León.* Edited by Victor Wolfgang von Hagen and translated by Harriet de Onis.
54. George E. Hyde. *Indians of the High Plains:* From the Prehistoric Period to the Coming of Europeans.
55. *George Catlin:* Episodes from "Life Among the Indians" and "Last Rambles." Edited by Marvin C. Ross.
56. J. Eric S. Thompson. *Maya Hieroglyphic Writing:* An Introduction.
57. George E. Hyde. *Spotted Tail's Folk:* A History of the Brulé Sioux.
58. James Larpenteur Long. *The Assiniboines:* From the Accounts of the Old Ones Told to First Boy (James Larpenteur Long). Edited and with an introduction by Michael Stephen Kennedy. Out of print.
59. Edwin Thompson Denig. *Five Indian Tribes of the Upper Missouri:* Sioux, Arickaras, Assiniboines, Crees, Crows. Edited and with an introduction by John C. Ewers.
60. John Joseph Mathews. *The Osages:* Children of the Middle Waters.
61. Mary Elizabeth Young. *Redskins, Ruffleshirts, and Rednecks:* Indian Allotments in Alabama and Mississippi, 1830–1860.
62. J. Eric S. Thompson. *A Catalog of Maya Hieroglyphs.*
63. Mildred P. Mayhall. *The Kiowas.*
64. George E. Hyde. *Indians of the Woodlands:* From Prehistoric Times to 1725.
65. Grace Steele Woodward. *The Cherokees.*
66. Donald J. Berthrong. *The Southern Cheyennes.*
67. Miguel León-Portilla. *Aztec Thought and Culture:* A Study of the Ancient Nahuatl Mind. Translated by Jack Emory Davis.
68. T. D. Allen. *Navahos Have Five Fingers.*
69. Burr Cartwright Brundage. *Empire of the Inca.*
70. A. M. Gibson. *The Kickapoos:* Lords of the Middle Border.
71. Hamilton A. Tyler. *Pueblo Gods and Myths.*
72. Royal B. Hassrick. *The Sioux:* Life and Customs of a Warrior Society.
73. Franc Johnson Newcomb. *Hosteen Klah:* Navaho Medicine Man and Sand Painter.
74. Virginia Cole Trenholm and Maurine Carley. *The Shoshonis:* Sentinels of the Rockies.
75. Cohoe. *A Cheyenne Sketchbook.* Commentary by E. Adamson Hoebel and Karen Daniels Petersen.

185

76. Jack D. Forbes. *Warriors of the Colorado:* The Yumas of the Quechan Nation and Their Neighbors.
77. *Ritual of the Bacabs.* Translated and edited by Ralph L. Roys.
78. Lillian Estelle Fisher. *The Last Inca Revolt, 1780–1783.*
79. Lilly de Jongh Osborne. *Indian Crafts of Guatemala and El Salvador.*
80. Robert H. Ruby and John A. Brown. *Half-Sun on the Columbia:* A Biography of Chief Moses.
81. *The Shadow of Sequoyah:* Social Documents of the Cherokees. Translated and edited by Jack Frederick and Anna Gritts Kilpatrick.
82. Ella E. Clark. *Indian Legends from the Northern Rockies.*
83. *The Indian:* America's Unfinished Business. Compiled by William A. Brophy and Sophie D. Aberle, M.D.
84. M. Inez Hilger, with Margaret A. Mondloch. *Huenun Namku:* An Araucanian Indian of the Andes Remembers the Past.
85. Ronald Spores. *The Mixtec Kings and Their People.*
86. David H. Corkran. *The Creek Frontier, 1540–1783.*
87. *The Book of Chilam Balam of Chumayel.* Translated and edited by Ralph L. Roys.
88. Burr Cartwright Brundage. *Lords of Cuzco:* A History and Description of the Inca People in Their Final Days.
89. John C. Ewers. *Indian Life on the Upper Missouri.*
90. Max L. Moorhead. *The Apache Frontier:* Jacobo Ugarte and Spanish-Indian Relations in Northern New Spain, 1769–1791.
91. France Scholes and Ralph L. Roys. *The Maya Chontal Indians of Acalan-Tixchel.*
92. Miguel León-Portilla. *Pre-Columbian Literatures of Mexico.* Translated from the Spanish by Grace Lobanov and the Author.
93. Grace Steele Woodward. *Pocahontas.*
94. Gottfried Hotz. *Eighteenth-Century Skin Paintings.* Translated by Johannes Malthaner.
95. Virgil J. Vogel. *American Indian Medicine.*
96. Bill Vaudrin. *Tanaina Tales from Alaska.* With an introduction by Joan Broom Townsend.
97. Georgiana C. Nammack. *Fraud, Politics, and Dispossession of the Indians:* The Iroquois Land Frontier in the Colonial Period.
98. *The Chronicles of Michoacán.* Translated and edited by Eugene R. Craine and Reginald C. Reindorp.
99. J. Eric S. Thompson. *Maya History and Religion.*
100. Peter J. Powell. *Sweet Medicine:* The Continuing Role of the Sacred Arrows, the Sun Dance, and the Sacred Buffalo Hat in Northern Cheyenne History.

101. Karen Daniels Petersen. *Plains Indian Art from Fort Marion.*
102. Fray Diego Durán. *Book of the Gods and Rites and The Ancient Calendar.* Translated and edited by Fernando Horcasitas and Doris Heyden. Foreword by Miguel León-Portilla.
103. Bert Anson. *The Miami Indians:* Sovereigns of the Wabash-Maumee.
104. Robert H. Ruby and John A. Brown. *The Spokane Indians:* Children of the Sun. Foreword by Robert L. Bennett.
105. Virginia Cole Trenholm. *The Arapahoes, Our People.*
106. Angie Debo. *A History of the Indians of the United States.*
107. Herman Grey. *Tales from the Mohaves.*
108. Stephen Dow Beckham. *Requiem for a People:* The Rogue Indians and the Frontiersmen.
109. Arrell M. Gibson. *The Chickasaws.*
110. *Indian Oratory:* Famous Speeches by Noted Indian Chieftains, compiled by W. C. Vanderwerth.
111. *The Sioux of the Rosebud:* A History in Pictures. Photographs by John A. Anderson, text by Henry W. Hamilton and Jean Tyree Hamilton.
112. Howard L. Harrod. *Mission Among the Blackfeet.*
113. Mary Whatley Clarke. *Chief Bowles and the Texas Cherokees.*
114. William E. Unrau. *The Kansa Indians:* A History of the Wind People.
115. Jack D. Forbes. *Apache, Navaho, and Spaniard.*
116. W. David Baird. *Peter Pitchlynn:* Chief of the Choctaws.
117. *Life and Death in Milpa Alta:* A Nahuatl Chronicle of Díaz and Zapata. Translated and edited by Fernando Horcasitas, with a foreword by Miguel León-Portilla.

LIFE AND DEATH IN MILPA ALTA is printed on paper which bears the watermark of the University of Oklahoma Press and which has an effective life of at least three hundred years.

University of Oklahoma Press

Norman